Seasons *of*
Central Pennsylvania

Seasons *of* Central Pennsylvania

A COOKBOOK BY

Anne Quinn Corr

THE PENNSYLVANIA STATE UNIVERSITY PRESS

UNIVERSITY PARK, PENNSYLVANIA

PUBLISHED IN ASSOCIATION WITH THE *Centre Daily Times*

STATE COLLEGE, PENNSYLVANIA

A KEYSTONE BOOK

A Keystone Book is so designated to distinguish it from the typical scholarly monograph that a university press publishes. It is a book intended to serve the citizens of Pennsylvania by educating them and others, in an entertaining way, about aspects of the history, culture, society, and environment of the state as part of the Middle Atlantic region.

Library of Congress Cataloging-in-Publication Data

Corr, Anne Quinn, 1950–
   Seasons of central Pennsylvania : a cookbook / by Anne Quinn Corr.
      p.   cm.
   Includes index.
   ISBN 0-271-02042-3 (cloth : alk. paper)
   1. Cookery, American. 2. Cookery—Pennsylvania. I. Title.

   TX715.C825 2000
   641.59748—dc21

                                     00–027722

Book design by Sigrid Albert
Printed in Canada

First paperback printing, 2001

It is the policy of The Pennsylvania State University Press to use acid-free paper for the first printing of all clothbound books. Publications on uncoated stock satisfy the minimum requirements of American National Standard for Information Sciences— Permanence of Paper for Printed Library Materials, ANSI z39.48–1992.

To Peter Amodei Baldwin, 1980–1998

Contents

Preface

In the fall of 1998 I attended a community workshop entitled "Restating Pennsylvania: Discussions on Our History, Culture, and Identity" held on the sweeping grounds of Centre Furnace Mansion, home of the Centre County Historical Society. It was a breezy Sunday afternoon in late September, and the trees rustled with the dry rattle of late summer. Fifty or so people were already seated under a canopy when I arrived at the last minute, just returning from a family camping trip where we enjoyed Penn's Woods to the fullest in the log cabins at S. B. Elliott State Park.

I listened to the end of the panelists' introductions and heard their thoughts about what it means to be a Pennsylvanian. For one person, it was the sweet scent of a newly mown hayfield. For another, it was the smell of chocolate in Hershey. Pennsylvania historian Bill Pencak related facts that made me more proud of Pennsylvania with each statement: how the state was a trendsetter, having no military presence for its first seventy-five years; how during those first seventy-five years it welcomed people from various parts of Europe; how it was an antislavery state; how it played a pivotal role in the newly developing American government, from its birth in Independence Hall until the national government was moved to Washington, D.C.; how the canals and railroads that traversed its challenging mountainous regions made it a forerunner in the transportation field; how the oil boom began in Titusville; how labor unions originated in Pittsburgh. The list continued. Combined with my euphoria from having spent the previous forty-eight hours literally in Penn's Woods, with each statement I felt myself puffing like a ruffed grouse, full of pride for my state.

Suddenly moderator Dr. Carla Mulford posed a question to the crowd: "How many present are native Pennsylvanians?" My hand shot up, along with the hands of about half those present. Wait a minute, I thought. My birth certificate reads Martin's Ferry, Ohio. I quickly dropped my hand. Then she asked, "How many are not?" and I lamely held my hand at half-mast.

Funny—I had never thought of myself as not a native Pennsylvanian. Here I am so proud of my state—and I'm technically not native. I'm a (gulp) Buckeye!

Unusual circumstances caused me to be born on the banks of the Ohio River. My mother was eight months pregnant when she received a telephone call informing her of the death of her father, a shot-fire man who set dynamite charges in a coal mine in southeastern Ohio. A ricocheting rock killed him. So, though my parents lived in Philadelphia, I came to be born in Ohio on the day my grandfather was buried, and I lived there for two months until my mother was able to travel back east.

Though not native-born to Pennsylvania, I am very close. My roots on opposite ends of the state have helped me to feel quite grounded here in the middle, in the town of State College, where I have lived since 1970. Straddling the state from the sophisticated and ethnic conclaves of Philadelphia to the simpler, earth-related focus of the rural folkways of the Ohio River valley, I have been granted an excellent vantage point right in the middle, digesting the best of both worlds.

Much of the discussion at the forum concerned sense of place and the unifying element that makes Pennsylvanians truly Pennsylvanians. For me, and I believe for many others, it is food. After all, we are basically just organisms continually seeking nourishment, in the hope of evolving. Our strongest memories come from foods prepared for us by our mothers, from smells that open the floodgates of emotion, from our visceral connection. We have become what we have eaten. When we eat from our environs, we become our environs in a most elemental way.

Approximately two-thirds of the recipes in this book have been published previously by the Centre Daily Times *during the fifteen years that I have been writing local food features. Many of the photographs have also already appeared there too. All this testifies to an abiding commitment to community journalism on the part of the* CDT. *This book would not have been possible without the support of the* Centre Daily Times*—not just because the* CDT *made the original photos available for reprint, but also in a more basic sense: If I had not had a deadline, these stories would never have been written in the first place.*

Writing for the Centre Daily Times *has been my opportunity to participate in the living journal of our times. Life here in Central Pennsylvania is very good—look at the crime statistics. People here care about one another—look at the announcements about service activities. And folks that live here take great delight in eating well—look at all the food features.*

In the brief spotlight my subjects enjoyed in the newspaper, I made note of the impact that their interests or special accomplishments have had in our community. This book will make those moments of glory less ephemeral and help them to reach a larger audience.

The recipes and article excerpts in these pages showcase the largesse of the state. Much of the raw material is available for the gathering or is easy to cultivate or obtain. The entire book is a celebration of the seasons and begins with fall, the inaugural period here. At that time a wave of new residents— mostly temporary, though many become rooted and never leave—flows into State College. Every September the town and surrounding environs become highly energized serving and assimilating that influx. This book will enable all those new or temporary residents to realize the extraordinary natural gifts of the region and to participate in the culinary communion that we share.

Acknowledgments

This book has been in progress for a long time, and many people I have encountered along the way have helped bring it to completion. The initial project was conceived during a conversation at Penn State Press with Patty Mitchell and Peter Potter, who have both been enormously helpful in realizing our mutual goal: to define and categorize the cuisine of the Central Pennsylvania region.

The Centre Daily Times, *through the generosity of publisher Lou Heldman, the photographic genius and diligence of Pat Little, and orchestration by Michelle Guisewhite, has been a collaborative partner in a large sense. Thanks, also, go to my headline-generating editors at the paper over the past fifteen years, especially the one with the most staying-power, Julie Brink, and to my current editors, Chris Arbutina and Jill Bedford.*

Other people who have helped along the way include Sigrid Albert, Janet Dietz, John Folse, Stacie Gutschall, Peggy Hoover, Elaine Light, Jean McKibbin, Jackie Melander, Nina Morgan, Shannon Pennefeather, Sara Pitzer, Kathy Ritchey, Pat Robison, Regina Ryan, and Ron Smith. For many of the portrait images in the book I am grateful to Alan Klein, a local photographer, who was most accommodating. For the scenery images, I am grateful to the State College Color Slide Club members, especially Lois Chavern, Marion Deppen, Tom King, Dennis Lamb, Elizabeth and Roger Pennock, and Carolyn Smith, for their extraordinary visuals. Many thanks for answering culinary questions and for recipe-testing go to Courtney Confer and Barbara Lange, who helped fine-tune the recipes. Thanks to my son Joe, my daughter Rose, and her friend Shazanna Shahrir for testing some of the recipes—even if they did not like all the ingredients!

I am most grateful to my subjects over the years and credit them for sharing their foodways with the general public. Truly, there would not be a book without them.

Finally, I am grateful to my husband, John, who knows more about the Commonwealth of Pennsylvania than anyone I know, and to our children, Joe, Alex, and Rose, who were patient and understanding with my commitment. I hope this book inspires them to maintain an appreciation of their native state and its wonderful gifts.

Introduction

Centre County offers a particularly appropriate vantage point from which to view Pennsylvania in terms of indigenous cuisine. Located right in the center of the Commonwealth, and surrounded by rural towns and countryside, it has become an island of regional specialties that make use of a fantastic natural abundance in time-honored ways.

The Pennsylvania State University draws sons and daughters of a vast number of the Commonwealth's citizenry into the area, bringing with them their own food preferences. International students create their own microcosms of diversity that are unmatched by any other geographic area of similar size in the state. A sophistication spurred by foreign travel, along with the entertainment demands of the university and local corporations, makes the cuisine of Central Pennsylvania well worth serious study and appreciation.

William Penn's letter to the Free Society of Traders in 1683 described the native population— the Lenni Lenape, or "Original People," as they called themselves—as generous and social:

But in Liberality they excel, nothing is too good for their friend; give them a fine Gun, Coat or other thing, it may pass twenty hands, before it sticks; light of Heart, strong Affections, but soon spent; the most merry Creatures that live, Feast and Dance perpetually; they never have much, nor want much: Wealth circulateth like the Blood, all parts partake; and though none shall want what the other hath, yet exact Observers of Property. Some Kings have sold, others presented me with several parcels of land, the Pay or Presents I made them were not hoarded by the particular Owners. . . . We sweat and toil to live; their pleasure feeds them, I mean, their Hunting, Fishing and Fowling, and this Table is spread every where; they eat twice a day, Morning and Evening; their Seats and Table are the Ground.

This inherently joyful approach toward food is alive today in Central Pennsylvania, as testified by the large number of outdoors experiences that are food related. Hunting season, fishing season, and game-bird season all bring significant numbers of people to the area to participate. The Lenni Lenape philosophy is still very much a part of the essential character of Central Pennsylvania, and put into practice by a great number of residents and visitors alike.

Indeed, "their pleasure feeds them."

Fall

Fall
Recipes

Fall

*F*all arrives with a flourish in Central Pennsylvania. The ennui of late summer is shattered with the first frost, shocking forest and garden with the threat of winter. Nature responds with a brilliant last hurrah, orange and red pigments blazing in trees and shrubs, truly one of the world's greatest natural displays.

Pennsylvania's biggest agricultural product can be found in an indigenous state and in glorious variety at this time of year. Mushrooms, for the trained woods sleuth who knows how to distinguish the edible and choice varieties from those that are toxic, are there for the gathering. A walk in the autumn woods can yield a chicken mushroom, with a taste far better than that of its namesake. Mysterious puffballs, some as large as soccer balls, appear overnight on mowed lawns, and a bloom of honey mushrooms on a dirt path in the woods looks like suede buttons sewn over the tree roots.

The smell of apples is in the air. At our house, one apple tree vaults the front yard, and two more in the back provide an abundance that never seems to quit. When you are in our house at this time of year, you know why the season is termed "fall." It's the apples—they land on the roof and roll down, dropping on the lawn to the delight of the many squirrels in our neighborhood, and to the dismay of *my husband, who doesn't like to see half-gnawed apples in the gravel driveway getting mashed any further. In the grass, the afternoon sun warms the fruit and creates a bee-busy carpet of intoxicating fragrance.*

In the backyard, birds hover near the Concord grape vine, plucking off the ripe fruit. On the slopes of Mount Nittany, winemakers Joe and Betty Carroll are busy picking and pressing, inviting friends and vintner wanna-bes to come and help them with the harvest of their award-winning wines.

At Harner Farm along Route 45, resplendent pumpkins dwarf the shrinking vines that nourished them, a riot of orange that never fails to bring a smile when passing. The search for the perfect pumpkin for the family is a matter taken seriously and can provide a fun afternoon, especially when the pumpkin is chosen directly from the field.

In communities throughout Central Pennsylvania, harvest festivals celebrate the change of season. Apples are pressed into sweet, amber rivulets of cider, and many towns stage community events that include apples in pies and dumplings, cakes and fritters, applesauce and apple butter. Pumpkin festivals delight young and old with edible treats and the wonder of seeing the biggest pumpkin in the area. Flaming-foliage festivals invite us to appreciate the splendor that is going on all around us, that changes daily, and that passes all too soon.

While there are many reasons to travel to Central Pennsylvania in the fall, the strongest magnetic force is oval and brown and covered with pigskin. Football brings nearly 100,000 revelers to Beaver Stadium for the home games. Flags and banners lend the air of a medieval pageant to the spectacular profusion of humanity that gathers in the fields surrounding the stadium. Win or lose, the show is always worth attending.

Halloween brings another kind of magic. By then the leaves have fallen and been raked into alluring piles that tempt youngsters to wade through them.

The humble porker—a proud symbol of State College attributed to an early photograph that shows a pig standing in the middle of what eventually became College Avenue—is in his prime at this time. Hog-butchering in the countryside provides succulent pork for roasts and stews. Hams are smoked to help preserve them the old-fashioned way and to infuse them with the seductive aroma of smoldering hickory.

November brings a chill to the air, and the last of the clinging leaves are blown away by a cold north wind. The Thanksgiving holiday brings families together around bounteous tables. Time for the prized jar of pickled peppers or corn relish or dilly beans to be retrieved from the root cellar.

Here in Central Pennsylvania a mighty legion is forming in the woods as hunters from all over the state and beyond gather at hunting camps for the annual deer harvest. The mostly male bonding ritual unites all participants as they provide sustenance for the year for their families by harvesting what many consider to be the most prized red meat in the world.

Aching brilliance of leaves vaults the forest,
shouts a crackling last hurrah,
while underneath the silent force
of mushrooms exhales earth's patois.

Wild Mushrooms

A mushroom walk with Bill Russell sharpens your senses. You learn to look for the barely perceptible, the mushrooms that nature camouflages into the landscape. A pile of rotting leaves? Look closer; a gyrodon bulges its dull tan cap. A tree stump? Maybe the other side is crowned with that orange jewel of the forest, the chicken mushroom. And there, in a clearing, tall and white against the brown forest floor (as if to say "Look at me! Look at me!"), stands the deadly amanita, or "angel of death."

"This is one of the best places in the country for wild mushrooms," says Bill, who makes the most of our local resource. Since 1960 he has held hundreds of mushroom workshops, often with longtime friend and fellow enthusiast John Haag, a poet and retired English professor.

Even armed with the best guidebooks, it is best to go mushroom hunting with an expert—and Bill Russell, with sixty years of experience, is an expert. Bill has been hunting mushrooms since he accompanied his Russian father and German mother into the fields as a toddler. The family gathered large quantities of white field mushrooms—similar to our cultivated button mushroom—to use in soups, stews, and sauces. Fully aware of the dangers of eating wild foods, Bill asserted his stance with a smile: "I have never been sick from eating wild mushrooms, nor has anyone ever gotten sick from mushrooms that I have given them. I would not give someone a mushroom that I have never tried myself. You can never be too careful."

A very special mushroom walk was held in 1990, with mushroom expert Bill Russell leading a WPSX-TV film crew that was working on a segment for "Outdoor Pennsylvania." Several area chefs were on hand in the woods to create the following dishes using the mushrooms that were found.

Bill Russell grins over a windfall of cinnabar chanterelles, and a Mushroom Pappardelle dish from Mario and Luigi's.

Maurice Philippet's Omelette with Chanterelles

SERVES 1 OR 2

Recipe by Maurice Philippet, then chef/ co-owner of The Victorian Manor, Lemont.

1 tablespoon clarified butter

1 teaspoon minced parsley

1 teaspoon minced garlic

½ cup fresh chanterelles (whole if small, chopped if large)

3 eggs, beaten

salt and pepper to taste

Heat clarified butter to the point of fragrance in a 9-inch omelette pan. Add parsley and garlic, and heat, stirring, for 15 seconds. Add the chanterelles and sauté quickly. When hot, add beaten egg and season to taste with salt and pepper. Agitate the pan by shaking and stirring the egg mass with a dinner fork without piercing the bottom. Fold and roll the omelette onto a hot plate when the eggs are cooked but still soft. The entire process should take about 90 seconds.

Remy Du Pasquier's Meatballs Forestière

SERVES 6

Recipe by Remy Du Pasquier, then co-owner of The Governor's Table in Bellefonte and chef at Café Atlantico in Washington, D.C.

1½ pounds ground beef

1 ounce black trumpet powder (made by drying and powdering black trumpet chanterelles to use as a seasoning)

salt and pepper to taste

¼ cup Burgundy wine

2 tablespoons cognac

2 tablespoons clarified butter for browning

SAUCE:

9 ounces fresh cèpes

4 ounces fresh boletes

2 tablespoons clarified butter

¼ cup chopped celery

¼ cup chopped carrots

¼ cup chopped radishes or shallots

1½ cups heavy cream

Combine beef with the black trumpet powder, salt and pepper, wine, and cognac and let sit, refrigerated, overnight. Shape into small balls and brown in 2 tablespoons clarified butter. In a separate pan, make sauce: Sauté the cèpes and boletes in 2 tablespoons clarified butter and add vegetables. When cooked, add the cream and reduce slightly. Add browned meatballs to the sauce and simmer until thoroughly heated.

Daniel Barbet's Seafood Sausages with Chanterelles and Cream Sauce

SERVES 2

Daniel Barbet, then owner of Le Gourmet Gourmand, a line of sausages, pâtés, and galantines, created many types of specialty sausages and marketed them to restaurants, hotels, and gourmet outlets across the country. Sausage is one of the original convenience foods—the word "sausage" derives from the Latin salsus, *meaning salted or preserved. Then, as now, natural casings were stuffed with seasoned meat and fat and stored or preserved and used as street food. The hotdog cart in front of the Corner Room has roots in Roman antiquity!*

3 tablespoons clarified butter

8 ounces seafood sausages (or substitute another type of mild gourmet sausage, such as veal or chicken)

½ cup white wine

1 cup chanterelles

1 teaspoon minced garlic

1 teaspoon minced parsley

1 cup heavy cream

   salt and pepper to taste

Heat 1 tablespoon clarified butter and sauté whole sausages until the casings start to brown. Remove the sausages and deglaze the pan with the wine. Reserve the pan drippings. Sauté chanterelles in remaining 2 tablespoons butter, then add the garlic and parsley. Cook briefly, then add the cream and the pan drippings and reduce until the sauce thickens slightly. Season to taste and pour the sauce over the sliced sausages that have been fanned out on the serving platter.

Daniel Barbet presents his specialty sausages.

Vietnamese Stir-Fried Noodles with Chicken and Wild Mushroom

SERVES 6

This was my own contribution to the feast into the woods, certainly a premier outdoor cooking experience under the canopy of the forest at Alan Seegar.

NUOC CHAM SAUCE:

2 cloves garlic

4 dried hot chili peppers

¼ lime, rind removed

4 tablespoons Vietnamese fish sauce (*nuoc mam*)

5 tablespoons water, or more to taste

2 tablespoons peanut oil

4 chicken thighs, skinned and boned and cut into thin strips

1 large red pepper, cut into julienne strips

2 leeks, cut into thin rings

1 pound rooting cauliflower mushroom, trimmed and cut into bite-size pieces

8 ounces rice-stick noodles soaked in warm water

Combine the ingredients for the sauce in a blender, process, and set aside. Heat the peanut oil in a wok. Add chicken and stir-fry until cooked. Remove chicken from the wok. Add the pepper, leeks, and mushroom and stir-fry for a few minutes. Drain the rice sticks and add to the wok, stirring to combine the ingredients. Add the cooked chicken to the noodle mixture and pour the Nuoc Cham Sauce on. Serve garnished with nasturtium blossoms.

Cook's Note

Any type of mushroom could be substituted for the rooting cauliflower mushroom. Area grocery stores now stock an enticing array of exotic mushrooms, and a mix of several varieties would be fine.

Tip

Unless they are very dirty, wiping mushrooms with a damp paper towel to remove visible dirt is the best way to clean them.

Edible Flowers

Roger Fisher's garden isn't large, but in scope it is enormous. Hand-dug, the 20 x 25 foot parcel of dark, organic earth supports a variety of herbs and edible flowers used for far more than making his carefully concocted dishes look beautiful. Roger's flowers also taste good. "Squash blossoms are very interesting dipped in a light tempura batter and deep-fried until crisp. Daylily blossoms can be stuffed with any number of creamy fillings, such as smoked tomato and cream cheese or a Boursin mixture," advised Roger. "The flowers of pungent herbs like oregano and mint have a more delicate flavor than the leaves and add an ethereal quality to a dish. And any green salad can be dressed up simply by adding some radishy nasturtium blossoms or lemony bergamot petals."

Roger has lived in the Centre Region since 1967, when he came to Penn State from Lower Burrell near New Kensington outside of Pittsburgh to study architecture. "When I first came to town, there were only a few hotels and several family-style restaurants," he recalled. "American food dominated. Today there is a lot of choice in the area for inventive cuisine, including new, small places with Indian, Japanese, Korean, and Mexican menus. Our population has become diverse, and demand for foods native to other countries has increased."

After working in many area restaurants and hotels, in 1988 Roger and then partner Remy Du Pasquier opened The Governor's Table in Bellefonte and operated the restaurant until 1993, when both moved on to other ventures. During the heyday of the enterprise, Roger found that he couldn't get the herbs he needed locally. With the help of his wife, Mary, a former agriculture student at Penn State, he started to grow his own. His garden is abundant with a wide variety of culinary herbs including nine varieties of thyme, five types of rosemary, three lavenders, and seven types of basil. The following recipes make use of his prodigious herbal bounty.

Roger Fisher delights in his garden of edible flowers and herbs.

Roger Fisher's Green Bean Salad

SERVES 4

1 pound green beans, trimmed and blanched

5 Roma tomatoes, chopped

1 Vidalia onion, chopped

3 tablespoons olive oil

1 tablespoon balsamic vinegar

  salt and pepper to taste

2 tablespoons fresh chopped Herbes de Provence blend including rosemary, tarragon, parsley, marjoram flowers, winter savory, lavender, and French thyme

  edible flowers for garnish

Combine blanched green beans, chopped tomatoes, and chopped onion and toss with oil and vinegar. Season with salt and pepper and sprinkle with the chopped herbs. Be sure to chop herbs as close to serving time as possible so their volatile oils are at their most pungent. Garnish salad with flowers.

Roger Fisher's Flower Tempura

SERVES 4

16 flowers, such as squash blossoms, dill flowers, fennel flowers, and elderberry and acacia blossoms

1 egg yolk

1 cup ice water

½ teaspoon spice mix (Roger uses his own 16-spice blend, but a mixture of allspice, cinnamon, and crushed fennel seeds to equal ½ teaspoon can be substituted)

1 cup flour

  peanut oil for deep-frying

  chutney for dipping (optional)

Prepare flowers (see Tip). Combine egg yolk and water. Mix the spices into the flour and cut the flour mixture into the liquid so that it is still floury and lumpy (a smooth batter is too heavy for a tempura). Pour peanut oil into a skillet to a depth of about 1 inch and heat over moderately high heat until it is hot (375°F). Quickly dip the flower into the tempura batter and place it in the hot oil, turning once when golden brown on the bottom to cook the other side. Remove with a slotted spoon and drain on paper towels on a baking sheet. These can be held for a short time in a 300°F oven but are best served immediately.

Tip

Pick flowers at mid-morning on a warm, dry day after the dew has evaporated and before the heat of the day. If using squash blossoms (any type will do—zucchini, yellow crookneck, pattypan, winter squash, pumpkin), remove the stamens or pistils, wash gently to remove insects, and pat dry. If using a cluster flower, such as dill or fennel, keep the whole head intact and dip quickly in cool water to rinse, then dry on paper towels.

The following two recipes were developed for a workshop that I presented to the Standing Stone Garden Club in Huntingdon. Even people who are very interested in flowers have often never tried to eat them. When they do, it is a memorable experience.

Nasturtiums Stuffed with Garlicky Gorgonzola Spread

MAKES 1½ CUPS

2 bulbs roasted garlic

1 teaspoon dried oregano

¼ cup buttermilk

8 ounces cream cheese

4 ounces Gorgonzola

nasturtium blossoms for filling

Squeeze the garlic from the roasted cloves and place into a food-processor bowl along with the rest of the ingredients. Process until uniformly smooth. Put filling into a pastry bag fitted with a star tip and pipe a small amount into the center of clean, dry nasturtiums.

Standing Stone Garden Club   September 15, 1998

The Visual Feast: A Workshop on Edible Flowers and
Presentation Tips
by
Anne Quinn Corr

Menu

Stuffed Nasturtium Blossoms
with Garlicky Gorgonzola Spread

Mesclun Salad with Edible Petals
and Nasturtium Vinegar Dressing

Vichyssoise with Borage, Lovage and Basil Blossoms

Scented Geranium Tea Bread

Anise Hyssop and Lavender Cookies

Lemon Curd Tartlets with Pansies, Impatiens and
Begonia Blossoms

Golden Mint Reception Punch

Menu for edible flowers workshop.

Cook's Note

For roasted garlic, see Baked Whole Bulbs of Garlic (page 100).

Scented Geranium Tea Bread

MAKES 1 LOAF

1 tablespoon butter

1 tablespoon superfine sugar

6 whole scented geranium leaves

2½ cups flour

¾ cup sugar

1 tablespoon baking powder

¾ teaspoon salt

½ cup scented geranium leaves, chopped

½ cup butter, melted

1 cup milk

½ cup vegetable oil

1 large egg, beaten

2 teaspoons vanilla extract

Preheat oven to 350°F. Butter a 9 x 5 inch loaf pan, sprinkle with superfine sugar, shake out the excess, and arrange two scented geranium leaves on the bottom of the pan. Sift flour, sugar, baking powder, and salt. Stir in the chopped scented geranium leaves. Combine melted butter, milk, oil, egg, and vanilla in a small bowl and mix.

Make a well in the center of the dry ingredients and add the wet ingredients, mixing lightly to combine. Fill the pan halfway with batter, then arrange the four leaves along the sides of the pan, sticking them into the batter. Pour remaining batter into the pan and smooth the top. Bake for 55 minutes, or until inserted toothpick comes out clean.

Cool tea bread on wire rack for 10 minutes, then remove from the pan and allow to cool completely on rack. Slice bread with a serrated knife into 15 slices and cut each slice into four triangles if desired. Arrange on a platter and garnish with more scented geranium leaves.

Football Weekend

Each home football weekend a tidal wave of humanity pours into the Centre Region from all directions. Temporarily anyway, the almost 100,000 people in the stadium on game day make the area the third-largest population center of the state, trailing only Philadelphia and Pittsburgh. The influx has a profound influence on the area's restaurants and hotels. Many area residents find themselves hosting out-of-town visitors in the fall, and simplifying the care and feeding of guests enables the host to join the festivities as well. Here are some football weekend feast menus. Enjoy!

Friday Night Menu
Barbara Lange's Mediterranean Seafood Stew*
Green Salad with French Dressing*
Oatmeal Bread**
Barbara Lange's Pear Frangipani Tart*

Saturday Morning Menu
Blueberry Muffins**
Melon Slices
Assorted Yogurts
Coffee and Tea

Saturday Afternoon Tailgate Menu
Marinated Filet of Beef with Horseradish
    Cream* and Crusty Rolls
Herb Dip* and Warm Penn State Cheddars
    Dip* with Vegetable Crudites
Norma Bayer's Honey Applesauce
    Oatmeal Cookies**
Tait Farm Apple Cider and Raspberry
    Shrub Punch**

Saturday Night Menu
Bluefish Baked in White Wine*
White Rice
Green Beans with Almonds
Sliced Tomatoes with Blue Cheese
Garlic Bread
Pam Harner's Blueberry Pie** with
    Penn State Creamery Vanilla Ice Cream

Sunday Morning Menu
Seth's Western Strata*
Slices of Ham or Bacon
Grange Shoofly Cake**
Fresh Fruit
Coffee and Tea

* Recipes follow.
** Recipes elsewhere in the book.

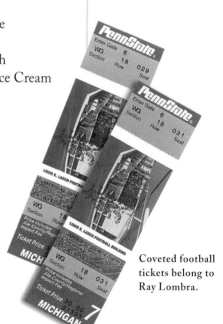

Coveted football
tickets belong to
Ray Lombra.

Barbara Lange's
Mediterranean Seafood Stew

SERVES 18

Barbara Lange chooses
fruit at the farmers'
market.

Barbara Lange came to Pennsylvania from Berkeley, California, in 1968 with her two small sons. "I'll never forget the train ride through Pennsylvania. It was June and so green that it seemed blue-green. We rode alongside the West Branch of the Susquehanna with the mist rising in the early morning, seeing fishermen, calm and focused. The mountain laurel was in full bloom and I had never seen anything so lush and beautiful." A visit to Centre County not long afterward convinced her to relocate to this area, where friends, like the Bell family that owned Nittany News, and the Buchanan family from Penns Valley, eased the transition for the young family.

Barbara has been an influential force in the culinary scene here ever since. From the early days as a charter member of the Downtown State College Farmers' Market, through the era when State College actually did have a natural foods restaurant, New Morning Café, Barbara has been involved—usually behind the scenes. She managed kitchens in Millheim at the hotel, in Bellefonte at the Gamble Mill Tavern, and in State College at Dante's. Her pastry skills are second to none, and I had the great fortune to observe this firsthand while we were partners in Q's Café, the first culinary operation at the Encore bookstore. My personal vision of heaven would be to have Barbara cook for me every day, to see her ceaselessly cheerful face and know that I could not possibly have it any better.

½ cup olive oil

3 cups leeks, chopped

2 cups onion, chopped

1 tablespoon garlic, chopped

½ cup celery, chopped

1 cup green pepper, chopped

1 bulb fennel, chopped

1¼ teaspoons turmeric

2 28-ounce cans diced tomatoes in juice

¾ cup tomato paste

1 teaspoon thyme

1 bay leaf

1 teaspoon fennel seeds

1 teaspoon cayenne pepper,
or more, to taste

6 cups clam juice, or vegetable or fish stock

1 pound medium shrimp, peeled,
shell removed, and deveined

1 pound scallops

1 pound crabmeat, picked over carefully
to remove shell and cartilage

1½ pounds firm-flesh fish (cod or pollack),
cut into 1-inch cubes

1 pint chopped clams and broth

1 tablespoon Pernod or Sambuca

salt and pepper to taste

In a large (12-quart) stockpot, heat oil and add leeks, onions, and garlic. Cook until translucent and then add the celery, green pepper, fennel, and turmeric. Cook, stirring occasionally, until the vegetables soften. Add remaining ingredients except for the seafood, and cook for about 20 minutes until it starts to boil. Reduce heat to a simmer or remove from heat until close to serving time. Add seafood to boiling liquid just before serving and stir to combine. Stew is ready when the seafood is cooked, about 5 minutes, or when the fish is opaque and the shrimp are pink.

Tip

The best way to pick crab is to dump out the container on a dark-colored tray, stand under a good light, and go through it a little bit at a time. You actually need to touch each bit because the cartilage is the same color as the crabmeat.

Cook's Note

The Chesapeake Blue Crab is esteemed as the most flavorful crab in the world. Our local watershed feeds into the Chesapeake Bay, and local groups like the Clearwater Conservancy and Trout Unlimited are always vigilant about preserving the crystalline quality of our headwaters.

Barbara Lange's Pear Frangipani Tart

SERVES 8 TO 12

This tart is delicious in the fall when local pears ripen, and Barbara uses pears from her own tree. Pear season tends to be overlooked here because of the preponderance of apples. When Larry Hammer took our apples to the press in Aaronsburg in 1998, he included a bushel or so of pears from his tree. The "mixed" cider was especially good.

Cook's Note

If the pears are not very ripe, they should be poached (after they are peeled, halved, and cored) in a solution of ¼ cup sugar to 1 quart water until they can be pierced easily with the tip of a knife.

Tip

Barbara slices the pears in very thin horizontal slices, then shingles the slices, keeping the pear half together.

1 10-inch tart pan with removable bottom, lined with pastry

½ cup unsalted butter

½ cup sugar

1 egg

1 tablespoon flour

2 cups almonds, toasted, cooled, and finely ground

3 tablespoons dark rum

1 teaspoon almond extract

3 to 4 pears, depending on size, very ripe

⅓ cup apricot jam

2 tablespoons Grand Marnier or other orange-flavored liqueur

Preheat oven to 375°F. Cream butter with the sugar until very light and very fluffy. Add the egg and the flour and continue to beat. Add the ground almonds, the dark rum, and the almond extract. Spread the mixture in the pastry shell and refrigerate while you prepare the pears. If the pears are very ripe, you need only peel, cut in half, and remove the core for each.

Slice the prepared pears and arrange in a decorative pattern on the top of the refrigerated mixture in the tart shell. Bake for 45 minutes, covering the top lightly with foil if it browns too quickly. Make a glaze for the tart by melting the apricot jam, straining it, and mixing in the liqueur. Use a pastry brush to apply the glaze to the top of the tart when it is finished baking. Allow to cool and then refrigerate.

Green Salad with French Dressing

SERVES 6

Like most children, my daughter Rose is far more apt to try something that she makes herself than something that just appears in front of her. She likes to make this simple French dressing— so unlike thick and sweetened bottled versions— for a salad of Boston lettuce and edible flowers.

3 tablespoons cider vinegar

1 tablespoon water

1 teaspoon Dijon mustard

½ teaspoon salt

½ teaspoon sugar

½ teaspoon pepper

½ cup sunflower oil

salad greens (for instance, Boston lettuce and edible flowers)

Combine all ingredients except the oil and greens in a two-cup jar and shake to blend. Add the oil and shake again to mix ingredients together. Shake well just before serving on clean, dried greens.

Herb Dip

MAKES 1 QUART

Serve with tiny broccoli florets, carrot slices, and celery sticks. This green sauce is also an excellent accompaniment to cold salmon.

2 cups spinach, washed and dried

1 bunch parsley, washed, dried, stems removed

2 bunches basil, washed, dried, stems removed

¼ cup onion, minced

2 tablespoons fresh lemon juice

1 tablespoon Worcestershire sauce

2 cups mayonnaise

1 cup plain yogurt

salt and pepper to taste

Place ingredients in food processor. Pulse and process until smooth.

Cook's Note

Find a small pumpkin at the farmers' market to hollow out for serving the dip. Use a large basket lined with kale leaves or doilies for displaying the vegetables. Nothing to wash!

Tip *(left recipe)*

For a side salad, plan on using about 3 ounces of greens (after cleaning) per person.

Marinated Filet of Beef with Horseradish Cream

MAKES ENOUGH FOR ABOUT 20 TO 30 SMALL SANDWICHES

This recipe has long been a standard at catered events. It is easy to prepare and has an aura of luxury. The Horseradish Cream sauce provides a creamy yet pungent foil for the savory beef.

5 pounds beef tenderloin, trimmed

MARINADE:

¼ cup soy sauce

¼ cup sherry

¼ cup water

4 cloves garlic, crushed

1 tablespoon ginger, freshly grated

1 tablespoon cracked black pepper

Tip

Trim the tenderloin, removing the "chain," a muscle that runs along the side. This can be slivered for use in stir-fry dishes.

Combine marinade ingredients and pour over beef in container, turning to coat the meat. Marinate for two days, flipping the meat over once or twice to coat all exterior surfaces with the mixture. Roast the meat the day before you want to serve it.

Preheat oven to 275°F (cooking at this low heat greatly reduces the amount of shrinkage). Remove meat from the marinade (discard the marinade). Place meat on baking sheet in center of oven and cook for 1 to 1½ hours, checking the meat occasionally with an instant-read thermometer. Remove roast when thermometer reaches 145°F. Allow to stand for a few minutes,

then slice beef in center to check the degree of doneness. If you want it less rare, return to the oven.

When done, chill beef rapidly in refrigerator, then wrap and reserve until serving time. At serving time, slice thin and arrange on platter. Serve at room temperature with crusty rolls and Horseradish Cream.

Horseradish Cream

1 cup heavy cream

½ cup prepared horseradish

Whip the heavy cream until thick and doubled in volume. Add horseradish and refrigerate until serving time. Makes 2 cups.

Warm Penn State Cheddars Dip

SERVES 16

This is another great dip for tailgates, if you are not serving additional cheese in your menu. The haunting flavor of the smoked cheddar makes it especially good in the fall and winter.

1 pound cream cheese, softened

½ pound sharp cheddar, grated

½ pound smoked cheddar, grated

vegetables for dipping

Combine the cheeses in food processor and process until smooth. Place in heat-resistant serving container and heat in microwave or conventional oven until melted and warm throughout, about 30 minutes in conventional oven at 375°F. Serve with blanched broccoli florets, cauliflower and broccaflower florets, carrot sticks, red-pepper chunks, or any other vegetables for dipping. Pretzel sticks also make a nice accompaniment.

Tip

An easy way to blanch the broccoli is to hold the stalk end and plunge the entire head into a saucepan of boiling water, count to 30, and then refresh in a bowl of ice water. The blanched florets are easy to trim off, and the peeled stalk makes a crunchy but mysterious addition to stir-fry dishes when the tops are missing.

Cook's Note

Penn State makes wonderful cheddar cheese in natural and smoked varieties. You can also purchase curds—small rounded bits of the cheddars for use in cooking—for less cost than the cheddar blocks and save yourself the trouble of grating.

Bluefish Baked in White Wine

SERVES 6

Cook's Note

To remove the skin from a fillet, place fillet on the work surface skin side down. Put the blade of the knife right between the skin and the flesh and run the knife down along the skin, separating the two.

Tip

This dish can be prepared in the morning and baked later in the day, after the football game is over!

Bluefish is the most common fish in the waters of neighboring New Jersey and is plentiful and relatively economical. Many people from the Centre Region vacation at New Jersey beaches, which are among the finest on the Atlantic Coast. Folks traveling to the shore can take an interesting detour to Fortescue, New Jersey, where former Stone Valley Outdoor School camp nurse Allen Will has a fishing-supply business at the marina. Allen sells bait and tackle at the shop on the Delaware Bay, as well as fish brought in by fishermen fortunate in the surrounding waters. This recipe could use any other type of firm-flesh fish, such as weakfish, a type of sea trout that is also native to the area.

2 tablespoons butter

1 medium onion, chopped in ¼-inch dice

1 carrot, chopped in ¼-inch dice

1 stalk celery, chopped in ¼-inch dice

¼ pound mushrooms, chopped in ¼-inch dice

salt and pepper to taste

½ cup dry white wine

2 pounds bluefish fillet, skinned

4 tablespoons minced fresh herbs
(any combination of parsley, chervil, tarragon, and thyme)

⅛ teaspoon paprika

Preheat oven to 425°F. Heat the butter in a frying pan and sauté the onion, carrot, celery, and mushrooms for 5 minutes, stirring often. Add the wine and parsley and cook for 2 minutes more. Butter or spray a large baking dish big enough to accommodate the fish in a single layer. Spread half the sautéed vegetables on the bottom, lay the fish on the vegetable bed, and cover with the remaining vegetables. Scatter the herbs over the top and sprinkle with paprika. Cover loosely with foil and bake for 20 minutes, or until the fish flakes easily with a fork.

Seth's Western Strata

SERVES 12

Scott Storll is a cook at the Gamble Mill Tavern who has a hot-sauce business on the side. Named after his young son, Seth, the business enables Scott to be a stay-at-home dad at least part of the time. Scott's wife, Sonia, works full-time as a physical therapist, and Scott is happy to take a significant role in child-rearing. Seth helps Scott in the garden, growing the various peppers for the three types of sauce—jalapeño for the green sauce, habanero for the fire sauce that is blended with mango pulp, and cayenne and serrano for the red sauce. Seth is not around, however, when the peppers are being processed. That is a spicy, heady job for Dad—and a powerful exhaust fan is required!

Seth's Hot Sauces debuted in 1998 and are available at specialty stores or through mail order. A versatile condiment, it can spice up your life.

Cook's Note

Remember to set the hot sauce on the table when serving so people who like a good morning burn can satisfy their needs.

Tip

Those who like their garlic more tame can sauté it a bit with the vegetables.

12 slices white bread

¾ pound sharp cheddar cheese

1 tablespoon butter

1 large onion, diced

1 large green pepper, diced

2 cups cooked ham, diced

2 large cloves garlic, chopped

3½ cups milk

½ teaspoon salt

6 eggs, slightly beaten

1 tablespoon Seth's Green Hot Sauce (or more or less, depending on personal preference)

3 ripe tomatoes, sliced, for garnish

Prepare a 9 x 13 inch baking dish by spraying or buttering it. Cut 12 doughnut-shape or fluted holes out of the bread and set aside. Chop the remaining bread scraps and place on the bottom of the prepared dish. Sprinkle the grated cheese over the bread.

Melt the butter in a sauté pan and cook the onions and peppers until tender. Add ham and mix. Place the vegetable-ham mixture on top of the cheese and arrange the reserved bread cutouts on top of the vegetables. Mix the garlic, milk, salt, eggs, and hot sauce together and pour over the assembly. Cover and refrigerate at least 6 hours or overnight.

Preheat oven to 350°F. About 1½ hours before serving, remove the strata from the refrigerator. Bake, uncovered, for 50 to 60 minutes, or until an inserted knife comes out clean. Allow to stand for 10 minutes before cutting and serving, garnished with the tomato slices.

Special-Occasion Indulgence

Leslie Shallcross adjusts a chocolate curl on her Cassata Cake.

Leslie Shallcross's full-dress Cassata Cake—with its crown of white and dark chocolate curls—is as wonderful in appearance as it is in taste. Rosettes of whipped cream and chocolate-dipped almonds provide the finishing touches. The cake itself is a genoise, a fine-textured sponge cake made with melted butter. Each delicate layer is soaked with almond liqueur then stacked with grated chocolate, chopped almonds, and whipped cream. Ricotta cheese adds substance to the whipped-cream frosting on the sides and top of this masterpiece. "Making the chocolate curls is the hardest part," says Leslie. "I spread melted chocolate on a rimless cookie sheet, then chill it until firm. Then I use a vegetable peeler to make the curls—if the temperature and the humidity cooperate."

A nutritionist, Leslie is trim and fit in spite of her proclivity for extraordinarily rich desserts. She believes that—unless you are on a restricted diet—it's not such a bad idea to consume so much cholesterol at one sitting, because the body can only absorb a certain amount of cholesterol at a time. How's that for justification?

Leslie Shallcross's Cassata Cake

MAKES 12 LARGE SERVINGS

At 650 calories per serving, this is hardly your everyday dessert. But for a very special occasion, it is as formal and fantastic a dessert as can be imagined—and worth every calorie.

6 slightly beaten eggs

1 cup sugar

1 cup flour

¼ cup unsalted butter, melted and cooled

3 tablespoons almond liqueur

3 tablespoons light rum

2 cups whipping cream

3 tablespoons powdered sugar

¼ teaspoon vanilla

3 1-ounce squares semisweet chocolate, grated

⅔ cup toasted almonds, finely chopped

¾ cup ricotta cheese, sieved

¼ teaspoon ground cinnamon

⅛ teaspoon ground nutmeg

additional whipped cream

chocolate-dipped almonds

7 ounces white chocolate

7 ounces dark chocolate

Preheat oven to 350°F. Prepare an 8-inch springform pan: butter and flour and line the bottom with a parchment circle. Combine eggs and sugar in a large mixing bowl. Place the bowl over a large saucepan of hot water (water should not touch the bottom of the bowl and should not boil). Heat over low heat, stirring frequently, for about 5 minutes, or until eggs are lukewarm. Remove from the heat. Beat egg mixture with an electric mixer on high speed for about 10 to 12 minutes, or until the mixture is thick and more than double in volume. Sprinkle the flour about a third at a time over the egg mixture and fold in gently. Fold in the melted butter.

Pour batter into prepared pan. Bake in the preheated oven for about 40 minutes until the cake tests done with a toothpick. Let cool in pan for 10 minutes, then remove from the pan and cool on a cake rack.

Combine liqueur and rum and set aside. Cut the cake horizontally into three layers. (For easier slicing, place the cooled cake in the freezer for 25 minutes before slicing.) In a large mixing bowl, combine the whipping cream, powdered sugar, and vanilla. Beat until soft peaks form. Place the first layer on a serving plate. Brush generously with the liqueur-rum mixture. Top with one-fourth of the whipped cream. Sprinkle with a generous tablespoon of chopped almonds and one-third of the grated chocolate. Repeat the procedure with the second layer. Top with the final cake layer.

Add the ricotta cheese to the remaining one-fourth of the whipped cream mixture and sprinkle in the cinnamon and nutmeg. Frost sides and top with ricotta mixture. Sprinkle the top with the remaining grated chocolate and press remaining chopped almonds into the sides of the cake. Chill several hours or overnight. At serving time, garnish the base with rosettes of whipped cream and chocolate-dipped almonds. Pile the chocolate curls on the top of the cake.

Chocolate curls: Melt 7 ounces each of white and dark chocolate and pour onto a rimless baking sheet, spreading to smooth it out. Chill until firm. Use a vegetable peeler to scrape up the curls.

Native American Touch

Nathan Benner holds the hook he used to capture his snapping turtle.

Many people in Centre County have a deep respect for the land that supports them. The Benner family is a clear example of the Native American philosophy that harmony with the environment is a key to the good life. Nathan Benner has been interested in Native American lifestyle and handicrafts for the past decade. He credits his father, Dave Benner, with awakening his appreciation of the outdoors.

Born and raised on the land where he lives, Dave hunts and keeps bees on his property in Zion. He notes the flowering of each species of tree and wildflower and uses a calendar to keep track of the information to determine where his bees are getting their nectar. Moonlighting from their day jobs, the father-and-son team also runs a pest-removal service to rid homeowners of skunks, possums, and other animals that find their way into civilized neighborhoods in the area.

When Nathan brought home two 15-pound snapping turtles, they worked together to clean them by putting the creatures in a barrel of rainwater for ten days, before butchering, extracting, and tenderizing the meat. In addition to some tasty dinners, Nathan, who has purchased turtle shells in the past, was pleased to get the shell, claws, and teeth for his Native American crafts, which he sells at powwows all over the state. Turtles held special significance for the Lenni Lenape of Pennsylvania, who believed that the Great Tortoise carries the island of the world on his back, much like Homer's Atlas.

Nathan Benner's Turtle Stew

MAKES 5 QUARTS

- 3 tablespoons bacon fat
- meat of 1 turtle, chopped
- 1 medium onion, chopped
- ½ cup celery, chopped
- salt and pepper to taste
- 1 cup carrots, chopped
- 1 cup corn, shucked from the cob
- 2 cups rice, cooked
- 3 quarts water or stock
- 1 tablespoon cornstarch, dissolved in ¼ cup water

Melt the fat in a heavy 5-quart soup pot and, when hot, brown the meat and the onion in it. Add celery, salt and pepper, and enough water or stock to cover all the ingredients in the pot. Let this simmer over a low heat for about 2 or 3 hours. Add carrots, corn, and cooked rice and simmer for another 45 minutes, adding additional water or stock as necessary. At the end of the cooking time, thicken if desired with the cornstarch-water mixture. Season to taste.

Snapper soup and turtle shell courtesy of Nathan Benner.

Author's Note

Growing up in Philadelphia under Bookbinder's influence, I always associated snapper soup with the taste of sherry. This version is quite different, though the texture of the meat is similarly chewy. Turtle meat is said to have the taste of seven meats—it has a unique flavor.

Tip

Adding a little of the hot stew to the cornstarch mixture first will keep it from forming lumps when it is incorporated.

Goose Day, September 29

East of State College, over the Seven Mountains Pass that separates Centre County from Mifflin County, the Juniata Valley provides a glimpse of a less hurried time with its many Amish settlements. Driving along the secondary roads must be done cautiously to bypass the horse-and-buggy vehicles. The very insulated communities guardedly maintain the old ways. Sometimes their traditions become mainstream for all the populace.

In 1973, local government officials in Lewistown, the county seat for Mifflin County, proclaimed Goose Day an annual event to be celebrated every September 29, recognizing a long-standing local custom. Rooted in traditions celebrated in the British Isles and in Holland, the legend maintains that if you eat goose on September 29 you will be $1,000 richer in twelve months. A history of Goose Day published by the Juniata Valley Chamber of Commerce in 1992 tells the story of a Pennsylvania Dutch farmer named Andrew Pontius who met a British navy man, Archibald Hunter, in Harrisburg in 1785 and hired him to be a tenant farmer. As was the custom in England, Hunter paid his annual rent on September 29, Michaelmas Day, the Feast Day of St. Michael and All Angels, and also brought his landlord a goose on that day to ensure good terms in the renewal of his lease.

Amish farmers bring their surplus geese to auction at the market in Belleville on Wednesdays, and Peachey's Market outside of Belleville takes advance orders for the birds. The holiday brings many people to Mifflin County to eat goose at church suppers and buffets held in halls of fraternal organizations that sponsor the community-wide event. Restaurants in both Mifflin and Juniata Counties have goose on the menu that day and do a booming business. It's common to hear the honking of the wild geese migrating from Canada to the Chesapeake Bay at this time of year, and the distinctive V-shaped flying formation is often seen in the sky, pointed south.

Roast Goose with Apples

SERVES 8

1 10-pound goose

8 apples, peeled, cored, and quartered

  salt and pepper

1 cup chicken stock

Preheat oven to 350°F. Rinse the goose and dry with paper towels. Remove visible fat from the bird. Season the cavity with salt and pepper and put the apple quarters inside. Puncture the skin of the goose in several places to allow the fat to run off during roasting. Place the goose on a rack in a shallow, heavy pan and roast it, allowing 20 minutes for each pound. A meat thermometer should register 165°F when the goose is done. With a baster, remove accumulated fat frequently during the cooking time.

Transfer to a warm platter and let rest, covered with foil, for 15 minutes before carving. Pour off the remainder of the fat, and add the chicken stock to the pan. Place over low heat to whisk the caramelized pan juices loose. Strain the liquid into a warm serving pitcher. Carve the goose, remove the apples, and serve with the hot juices poured over all.

Tip

Goose fat is highly prized as a cooking medium and is excellent to use for frying some potatoes to accompany.

John Koritko offers a game feast of wild birds.

Wild Birds

John Koritko's Stir-Fried Dove with Mushrooms and Peppers

SERVES 4

John Koritko, known to his friends as "Bucky," epitomizes what William Penn described when he said "their pleasure feeds them" in reference to the Lenni Lenape. Bucky has succeeded in turning a passion for game birds and hunting dogs into his livelihood as a national distributor for hunting-dog supplies based in Port Matilda.

A native of Uniontown, Pennsylvania, Bucky's lifelong passion for game birds and hunting dogs started when he was fourteen years old. Bagging six squirrels and a red fox his first time out hunting, he was hooked. Bucky and his wife, Janine Gismondi, an attorney, have two children and live in Fairbrook. A longtime member of the Ruffed Grouse Society, he also loves to cook his game in imaginative ways.

2 tablespoons butter

10 doves, breasts trimmed to fillets and cut into cubes

2 cloves garlic, crushed

1 cup mixed red and green peppers, cut into ¾-inch squares

1 cup mushrooms, sliced

½ teaspoon salt

½ teaspoon pepper

Heat butter in sauté pan until hot and stir-fry the dove-breast cubes and garlic for 3 minutes. Add peppers and cook for 2 minutes. Add mushrooms and cook for 1 minute. Serve with rice or noodles.

Tom Massaro's Grouse with Cinnamon and Walnut Sauce

SERVES 2

A local bird-dog enthusiast and member of the Ruffed Grouse Society, Tom Massaro uses the state bird in a tasty recipe.

- 2 tablespoons butter
- 2 grouse, breast filleted and cut into ¾-inch cubes
- 1 cup walnut pieces
- ½ cup raisins
- ¼ cup Madeira wine
- ¼ teaspoon cinnamon

Heat butter and sauté grouse cubes for 3 minutes. Add walnuts and raisins and sauté for 3 more minutes. Add Madeira and cinnamon and cook for 2 minutes, then serve.

Facts About Grouse

In 1931 the ruffed grouse was named the official state bird for Pennsylvania. Extensive logging at the turn of the last century had created an excellent habitat for the birds in brushy, logged-off forest areas. Today these areas have matured and the habitat is less supportive. Grouse are shy, and the expansion of the cities and towns has caused their range to shrink. This is especially visible in Centre County, where the population has been growing.

The Ruffed Grouse Society is dedicated to improving the environment for ruffed grouse, woodcock, and other forest wildlife. The Society works in conjunction with the Pennsylvania State Game Commission doing research, improving the habitat, and even acquiring land in the name of the state bird.

Fall game-bird hunting season draws many enthusiasts to the area, though the skill needed to apprehend these wary creatures is great indeed. One hunter remarked, after not even seeing a game bird during a five-hour hunt, "Oh, well, at least I got to spend the afternoon outdoors!"

The Vintner's Harvest

Betty and Joe Carroll lead
a fruitful life at Mount
Nittany Vineyards.

Betty Carroll's
Steamed Salmon in White Wine

SERVES 4 TO 6

Joe and Betty Carroll's 60-acre farm undulates down the southern slope of Mount Nittany toward Brush Valley Road. Four acres planted with grapes surround a stone winery, whose inviting upper deck overlooks the valley. The Carrolls purchased the land in 1983, planted fruit the following year, and were producing by 1988. Self-taught viticulturist Joe said they did a few things right. "First we named it Mount Nittany Vineyard and Winery, and that was a good move. We came up with our Tailgate Red wine, which is very popular in the fall. Since we are now the only winery in Centre County, we're popular with visiting alumni. And we are blessed with good land, a farmer's foremost concern."

September is a busy time at the winery, with dozens of friends and other volunteers harvesting the grapes. For a unique Centre County experience, visit the winery and taste the award-winning wines.

1 2-pound fillet of salmon

1 cup dry white wine

¼ cup fresh dill, chopped

¼ cup fresh parsley, chopped

   freshly ground pepper

1 lemon, sliced

Preheat oven to 375°F. Place salmon on a rack in a baking dish over a small amount of water to which 1 cup of wine has been added. Season fillet with slices of lemon, the dill, and the parsley and pepper. Cover the entire dish with aluminum foil and place in hot oven for 20 to 25 minutes. Serve with glasses of white wine.

Tip

Always use the lesser amount of time when cooking fish. The delicate proteins will continue to cook after the dish is removed from the oven, and overcooking toughens the finished product.

Apple Time

Corene Johnston plucks an apple at Harner Farm.

Corene Johnston—cook, goatherd, poet, jeweler, nurse practitioner, writer, and friend—is an extension of the very earth beneath her feet. She has taught me more about tuning in to the seasons and welcoming them with joy than anyone else I have known.

Corene celebrates every season with commendable vigor. Easter celebrations on Sparks Street were Old World, filled with dyed eggs and festive breads. Fragrant, cinnamon-spiced Christmases in her Coleville home treated friends old and new to three rooms full of holiday food and thoughtful little gifts. In summer, Corene gardened and delighted in every gift the earth gave back as reward. Zucchini and eggplant were transformed miraculously into ratatouille, berries burst into pies and shortcakes, beans and cucumbers were pickled and prized.

But autumn is her season of power. Her apple-butter-making harvest festivals bring scores of friends out to her hard-won and now comfortably appointed homestead—Champagne Cork Farm on Moose Run Road, where she and her husband, poet John Haag, live. After hours of peeling and cutting and stirring and snacking, she slices loaves of warm whole-grain breads and slathers them with apple butter hot from the kettle. Music and laughter echo through the folds of her very own Appalachian Hollow, ringing clear under an orange harvest moon.

Corene Johnston's Apple Butter Dip

MAKES I CUP

½ cup apple butter

½ cup spicy brown mustard

Mix, cover, and let stand at room temperature a few hours before serving. Delicious served on a cheese tray or with soft pretzels.

Corene Johnston's Apple Butter Sour Cream Cake

MAKES TWO 4 X 8 LOAVES

¼ cup butter

1 cup honey

½ cup white or turbinado sugar

3 eggs

2 teaspoons vanilla

1 cup sour cream

1½ cups unbleached white flour

1¼ cups whole-wheat flour

1 teaspoon baking soda

1 teaspoon baking powder

1½ teaspoons cinnamon

½ cup plus 2 tablespoons apple butter, without sugar or spices

Preheat oven to 325°F. Prepare two 4 x 8 inch loaf pans by generously buttering them or spraying with cooking spray. Cream the butter, honey, and sugar together. Beat the eggs in one at a time, then add the sour cream. In a separate bowl, combine the white flour, wheat flour, baking soda, baking powder, and cinnamon. Fold the dry ingredients into the egg mixture.

Pour one-quarter of the batter into each of the prepared pans. Divide the apple butter between the two pans and use a knife to swirl it into the batter, marbling the mixture. Top with the remaining batter, then swirl 1 tablespoon of apple butter into the top of each cake. Bake at 325°F for 30 minutes, then reduce the heat to 300°F, and bake for another 30 minutes, or until a toothpick inserted comes out clean. Cool for a few minutes in the pans, then remove pans and let the cakes cool on a wire rack. These cakes freeze well and taste best when made 24 hours before serving.

Cook's Note

This cake is high in calories and saturated fat and should be reserved for rare, special occasions. If the occasion is rare enough, you can throw all caution to the wind and top each slice with a dollop of whipped cream or a scoop of ice cream.

Apple Crisp

SERVES 4, OR MAKES UP TO 36 BITE-SIZE TASTES

This recipe is in the lab manual for nutrition and hotel, restaurant, and institution management students at Penn State University. The students enjoy making it because it is not only edible—unlike some experiments in the lab—but also tasty. I've heard reports that this is the recipe most likely to be duplicated in their apartment kitchens, to the raves of delighted roommates. The crisp can be baked in the microwave, which is very fast, or in a conventional oven, which makes it much crisper, or both—which often saves the day in the lab when it is not ready in time.

3 cups cooking apples, quartered, cored, peeled, and sliced (use Northern Spy, Granny Smith, McIntosh, Rome, or Empire)

¼ cup raisins

½ cup brown sugar, divided

½ cup whole-wheat flour

¼ cup oatmeal

¼ cup butter

¼ teaspoon cinnamon

¼ cup walnuts, chopped

If using a conventional oven, preheat to 375°F. Blend apple slices with the raisins and ¼ cup of the brown sugar. Place mixture in a 1-quart casserole dish. Blend flour with remaining ¼ cup brown sugar and cut butter in until coarse crumbs form. Stir in oats, cinnamon, and nuts. Press topping mixture onto surface of apples but do not stir. Bake in preheated oven for 40 to 45 minutes, or until the apples are tender. Alternatively, microwave on high for 8 minutes.

Pumpkins and Winter Squash

Pumpkin recipes are
popular in the fall.

Pumpkin Soup

SERVES 8

This is an adaptation of a Native American recipe I used many times in the elementary schools while doing cooking demonstrations. The students always enjoyed it because they made it themselves right in the classroom. We used to scoop out a pumpkin and clean and toast the seeds, then serve the soup from the pumpkin "tureen" and garnish each serving with the toasted seeds.

> 1 large can (29 ounces) pumpkin
>
> 1 quart milk
>
> 2 tablespoons butter
>
> 2 tablespoons honey
>
> 2 tablespoons maple syrup
>
> ½ teaspoon marjoram
>
> 1 teaspoon salt
>
> ¼ teaspoon white pepper
>
> ¼ teaspoon cinnamon
>
> ¼ teaspooon nutmeg
>
> juice of 1 orange

Heat pumpkin, milk, butter, honey, and maple syrup together slowly in large saucepan. Combine marjoram, salt, white pepper, cinnamon, and nutmeg and stir into pumpkin-milk mixture. Heat slowly, stirring, to simmering point. Do not allow to boil. Add the orange juice, a little bit at a time, stirring constantly. Serve hot.

Tip

If you plan on serving the soup from a hollowed-out pumpkin, it will stay warmer if you run hot water in the pumpkin to heat it before adding the hot soup.

Marcia Thompson's Microwave Pumpkin Oatmeal

SERVES 2

Former Penn State grad student Marcia Young Thompson makes this hearty breakfast recipe that cooks in minutes in the microwave. Adding pumpkin to your diet at any time gives you a nutritional boost. Don't wait for pumpkin pie.

> 1 cup oatmeal
>
> 2 cups water
>
> ½ cup pumpkin
>
> ¼ teaspoon cinnamon
>
> brown sugar or maple syrup, to taste
>
> raisins or other fruit (optional)

Cook oatmeal in water on high setting for 2 minutes. Stir, add one-quarter of the pumpkin, and continue cooking for 1 more minute. Add remaining pumpkin, stir, and sweeten to taste with brown sugar or maple syrup. Add raisins or other fruit if desired.

Kirstin Kapustik's
Pumpkin Chocolate Chip Cake

MAKES 2 LOAVES

Children's first forays into the kitchen often involve baking. By making these positive experiences and reinforcing them, a parent can nurture a lifelong love of cooking and culinary self-reliance. My friend Kirstin Kapustik, daughter of Tom and Gina Kapustik of State College, started making this recipe when she was twelve years old. An accomplished pianist and ballerina, Kirstin is gifted in many ways. Lucky to have a mother who enjoys cooking and a father who enjoys eating (I wonder which came first), she is also at ease in the kitchen. Gina makes these in cupcake shapes for little sister Natalie's birthday parties at school.

3½ cups flour

1½ teaspoons salt

1 teaspoon nutmeg

1 teaspoon cinnamon

3 cups sugar

2 teaspoons baking soda

1 cup oil

⅔ cup water

4 eggs, beaten

1 16-ounce can pumpkin

1 12-ounce package chocolate chips

GLAZE:

⅓ cup butter

2 cups powdered sugar

1½ teaspoons vanilla

2 to 4 tablespoons hot water

Preheat oven to 350°F. Prepare two large or three regular-size loaf pans by spraying with nonstick cooking spray or grease. Into a large bowl, sift together flour, salt, nutmeg, cinnamon, sugar, and baking soda. In a smaller bowl, combine oil, water, eggs, and pumpkin and mix well. Make a well in the center of the dry mixture and add the liquid mixture and the chocolate chips. Stir together to combine. Divide into prepared pans. Bake for 1 to 1¼ hours, or until pick inserted near the center comes out clean. Cool on wire racks set over a baking sheet.

Glaze: Heat butter until delicately golden. Blend in powdered sugar and vanilla. Stir in hot water until desired consistency is reached. Drizzle over cooled cakes on baking tray and allow the glaze to harden.

Wild Mushroom Lasagne with Butternut Squash Filling

MAKES 12 MAIN-COURSE OR 24 SIDE-DISH SERVINGS

This is a casserole version of the popular Butternut Squash Ravioli served at the Gamble Mill Tavern in Bellefonte. There isn't anything low-fat about it, and it is worth every calorie.

SQUASH FILLING:

4 pounds butternut squash, cubed

2 tablespoons butter

salt and pepper

1 tablespoon crumbled sage

MUSHROOM SAUCE:

½ cup butter

2 pounds mixed exotic and domestic mushrooms (button, shiitake, cremini, and oyster)

2 tablespoons brandy

1 quart heavy cream

salt and pepper to taste

WHITE SAUCE:

½ cup butter

½ cup flour

3 cups milk

4 egg yolks

grated Parmesan cheese

bread crumbs

1 pound spinach pasta sheets

Make squash filling: Preheat oven to 400°F. Cut squash in half and bake with cut-side down until soft and caramelized around the edge, about 40 minutes. Cool. Scoop out the flesh and mash with butter and seasonings. Cook in top of a double boiler to dry out the mixture. Stir frequently. Reduce heat to 350°F.

Make mushroom sauce: Melt butter and sauté mushrooms over moderately high heat. When they are soft, flambé with the brandy. After the flame subsides, add enough heavy cream to cover the mushrooms. Boil until cream is reduced by half and thickened. Season with salt and pepper.

Make white sauce: Melt butter and whisk in flour. Cook just until the flour starts to turn light golden brown. Gradually add milk and whisk until mixure is smooth and thick. When it comes to a boil, remove from heat and add 2 tablespoons of the hot white sauce to the beaten egg yolks to warm the yolks, then add the warm yolks to the white sauce.

Spray a large casserole (4-liter Pyrex baking dish) with nonstick cooking spray. Layer mushroom sauce, uncooked pasta, squash, pasta, mushroom sauce, pasta, squash, pasta, mushroom sauce. Top with white sauce and sprinkle with grated cheese and bread crumbs. Bake at 350°F for 1 to 1½ hours, or until top is golden brown. Let rest for 15 minutes before cutting to serve.

The Noble Porker

John Ziegler, retired professor of food science at Penn State, is a past Pennsylvania Pork Cookout King with valuable insight on the subject of pork. New breeding techniques produce animals with increased muscle and decreased fat. "Pork is an extremely interesting case today because it is still considered a fat, red meat by most consumers; however, many cuts of pork are as lean or leaner than many items of red meat, poultry, and seafood." During the Middle Ages it was difficult to keep a pig throughout the winter, so Europeans had an annual tradition of butchering the family pig at the end of the year. This tradition evolved into a village ceremony of feast and work that continues today in many rural areas. Pork became a staple of the winter diet—the cassoulets of France, the sauerkraut dishes of Germany, the rich stews of Poland—and every part of the animal was used. Central Pennsylvania has long been a big producer of pork, and many fine recipes originated here too.

Raspberry Pork Tenderloins

SERVES 4

2 pork tenderloins, about 8 ounces each

½ cup Tait's Raspberry Shrub, or any other shrub variety

2 tablespoons oil

2 shallots, chopped

¼ cup minced fresh herbs (parsley, thyme, savory, rosemary)

   salt and pepper to taste

1 cup chicken stock

   Tait Farm Fresh Raspberry Mango Salsa (see Summer, page 194)

Marinate pork tenderloins in shrub for 4 hours or overnight. Preheat oven to 300°F. Remove meat from the marinade and reserve the marinade for the sauce.

Heat the oil in a sauté pan until hot, then add the chopped shallots. After a minute or so, sear the tenderloins in the hot oil, turning frequently. When brown on the outside, place the pork in a roasting pan and finish cooking in the oven for 15 or 20 minutes. Add the chicken stock to the pan drippings and deglaze. Add the minced herbs, and season the liquid with salt and pepper. Add the reserved marinade and cook the sauce for a few minutes, reducing it to about half its original volume. Strain the sauce to remove the solids and keep warm.

Remove the pork from the oven when it registers 140°F on an instant-read thermometer. Allow the pork to rest for a few minutes, tented with foil. Carryover cooking will raise the internal temperature without overcooking the meat. The final temperature should read 155°F. Slice thinly and pour on the warm sauce. Serve with Tait Farm Fresh Raspberry Mango Salsa as a savory relish on the side.

Cook's Note

Tait's Shrub is available at local specialty stores. If it is not available, you can substitute a mixture of ¼ cup honey and ¼ cup raspberry vinegar.

Jeanne Confer's Ham Potpie

SERVES ABOUT 12

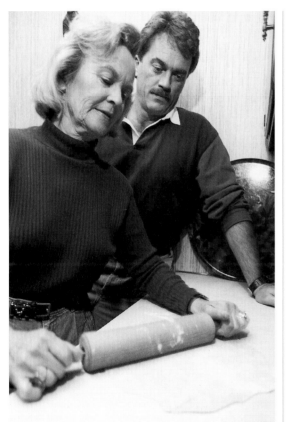

A mother-son team,
Jeanne and Courtney
Confer, make ham potpie.

Church suppers featuring ham potpie dominate in late fall, when the hogs are being butchered. This popular comfort food is a regional specialty that strikes a gustatory nerve in all who grew up in the area. Nothing like the Pennsylvania Dutch pastry-topped potpie, ham potpie is a noodle dish that has very simple ingredients and takes most of the afternoon to prepare. Like most country dishes, it is dependent on using a top-quality hickory-smoked ham like that produced by Hosterman's Market in Centre Hall. Courtney Confer, chef-owner at the Gamble Mill Tavern in Bellefonte, is my culinary counselor in all local traditions, having grown up in rural Penns Valley. In spite of having a highly developed and sophisticated palate, Courtney is satisfied with nothing else but the ham potpie made by his mother, Jeanne Confer, for his birthday dinner every September. Nothing else will do. Typical side dishes are pickled beets and a sweet-and-sour cabbage slaw studded with celery and caraway seeds.

1 5- to 7-pound butt-end ham, preferably
   from Hosterman's in Centre Hall
1 medium onion, chopped
2 12-ounce cans low-sodium chicken broth
1 cup parsley, chopped
   potpie noodles

Place ham in large pot, cover with water, and bring to a boil. Cook for 10 minutes, drain off the water, and discard. This step reduces the salt from the cure used in smoking the ham.

Place the ham in a roasting pan and bake at 350°F for about 1 hour.

Then put the ham back into the large pot, cover it with water, and place on stovetop. Add the chopped onion and simmer for another hour, or until it tests tender with a fork. Remove ham from the pot of broth and cool the meat so it can be taken off from the bone. Dilute ham broth with the low-sodium chicken broth to reduce the saltiness.

Potpie Noodles

- 4 or 5 eggs
- ¼ cup water or milk
- 4 cups flour
-   a few grinds of fresh pepper

Beat the eggs together and add the water or milk. (Jeanne uses the water, but her mother used to make it with milk.) Gradually add the flour one cup at a time, stirring it into the liquid until it forms a dough. Season with a few grinds of fresh pepper. Divide dough in half and roll out on a large, floured surface as thin as possible. Cut into 1½-inch squares.

Bring the broth to a boil and add the noodles a few at a time. The noodles will double in size when cooked. Reduce the heat so the broth is at a simmer and cook the noodles for about 1 hour. Cut the ham into chunks and add to the pot of cooked noodles right before serving time, along with the chopped parsley.

Note: Many people add potatoes to their potpie, although the Confer variation omits it because Jeanne grew "tired of everyone picking around the potatoes to eat the ham and noodles." If you want to add them, peel and slice five potatoes and add them when the noodles are cooking.

Author's Note

I've had people come up to me and say, "Potpie? It's only a big wad of dough." All I can say is that they didn't have a good batch. This is the recipe for the real thing.

Jeanne Confer's Cabbage Slaw

SERVES 12

- 6 cups cabbage (a small head), grated
- 2 carrots, grated
- ½ cup red pepper, minced

CELERY SEED SLAW DRESSING:

- 2 tablespoons sugar
- 1 teaspoon dry mustard
- 1 teaspoon salt
- ¼ cup apple-cider vinegar
- 1 cup mild salad oil
- 2 teaspoons celery seeds
- 1 teaspoon caraway seeds

Mix all dressing ingredients in large bowl, then add the vegetables. Toss thoroughly to combine.

Courtney Confer's Mountain Stew

SERVES 24

This is the traditional Friday night meal for the extended Corr family's annual camping trip, when we head to the cabins of S. B. Elliot State Park. Pennsylvania's state park system is one of the finest in the world, and the cozy log cabins built in the 1930s by the Civilian Conservation Corps give Pennsylvanians access to the woods at a very reasonable cost. There is nothing more restorative than the smell of this stew simmering on the woodstove in the cabin and the sound of rustling leaves as the cousins run around the campground greeting the families arriving at our mountaintop getaway. This is an industrial-size recipe for a big crowd.

¼ pound bacon, diced

4 cups onion, diced

1 cup celery, diced

3 pounds kielbasa, cut into ½-inch slices

4 quarts chicken stock

1 teaspoon cracked black pepper

8 carrots, peeled and sliced

4 parsnips, peeled and sliced

1 large rutabaga, peeled and cubed

4 turnips, peeled and cubed

8 potatoes, cubed

1 cabbage, coarsely chopped

   salt and pepper

1 cup chopped fresh parsley

Brown bacon, add onion and celery, and cook for a few minutes until they soften. Stir in kielbasa and sauté. Add stock and pepper and simmer, covered, for 20 minutes. Add carrots, parsnips, rutabaga, turnips, and potatoes. Simmer, covered, for about 40 minutes. Add cabbage and cook for another 30 minutes, adding more stock to cover all the vegetables, if necessary. Season with salt and pepper and add fresh parsley at serving time.

International Sharing

Fall is the time at Penn State to get involved with the new international students as they acclimate themselves to life in America. When I think of how lonely I was when I first came to the main campus from Abington Campus, I can just imagine how someone who is away from their family, friends, and any familiar landmark feels. The Community International Hospitality Council (CIHC) offers an opportunity to meet people from all over the world.

The first time we met Durga and Ganesh Rauniyar they came to our home for dinner. It was February 1986 and I was just home from the hospital with our new daughter, Rose. When I opened the door to greet them I saw a beautiful woman with wide eyes, like a deer caught in the headlights, holding a tiny baby—daughter Jyoti. Durga, resplendent in a golden sari, ventured a hesitant smile. While our husbands went off doing guy things, we bonded. Spreading a satin coverlet on the floor, we laid our babies down together and compared the two—one golden and long, one pink and round, two beauties, born six weeks apart on opposite ends of the earth, yet together, then and there. We have remained steadfast friends ever since.

In the CIHC program, local "friendship families" are matched with international families, and singles with international singles, of similar interests whenever possible. There are always more international students needing hosts than the other way around. I don't know what other hosts do with their students, but most of our interactions involved food. Whether at our house or theirs, we were always discussing crops and preparation, ingredients and presentation. We learned from each other in a memorable, flavorful manner.

Though similar to Indian cuisine, Nepalese food is not as spicy and is generally simpler. It is also lighter because it is prepared with less oil. Mustard-seed oil is the most commonly used cooking oil in Nepal, though any oil can be substituted. The following chicken recipe was our family's favorite from Durga's repertoire.

Durga Rauniyar's
Nepalese Chicken *(Kukhura ko Masu)*

SERVES 8

Cook's Note

Garam masala is a mixture of fragrant spices. Durga used a masala that Ganesh's mother had given her. To make your own, toast the following spices in a 250°F oven for 20 minutes, then grind:

one 3-inch piece of cinnamon

¼ cup green cardamom pods

2 tablespoons each of whole cloves, whole cumin, and whole coriander

1 tablespoon whole black pepper

Tip

If you enjoy Indian or Nepalese cooking, invest in a coffee grinder that you reserve for grinding spices. It is the perfect tool for creating your own signature masala.

4 pounds chicken thighs, skin removed, bone left in

6 tablespoons plain yogurt

¼ cup cooking oil

3 whole cloves

3 whole bay leaves

4 medium onions, cut in thin slivers

4 to 5 cloves of garlic, minced

1-inch cube of fresh ginger, grated

3 cardamom pods

1½ teaspoons cinnamon powder

2 tablespoons garam masala or curry powder

½ teaspoon turmeric

salt to taste

3 fresh tomatoes, chopped, or 3 tablespoons tomato paste

⅓ cup fresh cilantro, chopped, for garnish

Marinate chicken in yogurt overnight in refrigerator. Heat oil in a large, wide pot and add cloves and bay leaves to season the oil. Sauté onion in oil until transparent, then add garlic, ginger, and all the spices and salt. Cook for 2 minutes. Add chicken and sauté until browned and crisp on the outside. Add tomatoes or tomato paste and cook until chicken is thoroughly done, about 30 to 40 minutes. Water can be added if the dish is too dry. Garnish with the fresh cilantro at serving time.

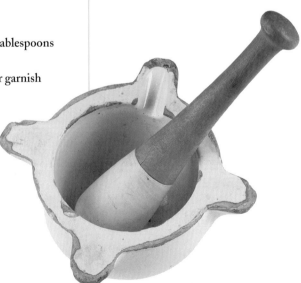

Durga Rauniyar's Mung Bean Soup

(Moong ko Dal)

SERVES 8

1 cup mung beans, rinsed

1 teaspoon butter

1½ quarts water

½-inch cube ginger, grated

1 clove garlic, minced

½ teaspoon turmeric

2 to 3 medium tomatoes, chopped

salt and pepper to taste

Wash mung beans and rub with butter. Combine with remaining ingredients and cook until beans are tender, about 45 minutes. Season with salt and pepper.

Durga Rauniyar's Cucumber Pickle

(Kankro ko Achar)

SERVES 8

2 medium cucumbers, peeled and seeded

salt

4 tablespoons sesame seeds

juice of 2 to 3 lemons

cayenne pepper

2 teaspoons oil

1 teaspoon fenugreek seeds

½ teaspoon turmeric

Chop cucumber into ½-inch dice, sprinkle with salt, set aside to drain for 30 minutes, then pat dry. Toast sesame seeds in a dry sauté pan until brown. Combine toasted sesame seeds, lemon juice, and pepper in blender and blend for 30 seconds. Pour the liquid over the prepared cucumbers, stir to coat. Heat oil and sauté fenugreek seeds until they turn black. Add turmeric and immediately remove from heat. Pour on the cucumbers and serve.

Michel and Nathalie
Fraisse enjoy dinner in a
local wine cellar.

From 1989 to 1991, I was fortunate to have a special person in my life who had a tremendous influence on my cooking style. Nathalie Longefay, in the United States while her fiancé, Michel Fraisse, worked on his MBA degree, is a native of the hills of the Beaujolais region in France, which resembles Central Pennsylvania in terrain, though the hills there are lined with grapevines instead of corn rows. We spent countless hours in the kitchen together, comparing two similar but distinct methods, as we prepared food for hundreds of special events. When I finally had the opportunity to visit Nathalie in France and was treated to her mother, Denise, standing at the stove in her country kitchen preparing dishes Nathalie had told me about, I understood why she was so connected with her cuisine. French people have a fine respect for food and enjoy their meals in a way that seems to be slipping away in America. Nathalie always appreciated the new foods we would experiment with, and remarked that we are so lucky here because we have so many types of food from which to choose. In France, she lamented, it is only French food.

Nathalie Longefay's Sausages and Shallots Cooked in Beaujolais

SERVES 4

The third Thursday in November marks the release of the Beaujolais Nouveau, or new wine, which is a fresh and fruity light red wine bottled four to six weeks after the harvest with flavor characteristics of peaches and roses. Nathalie's cousin produces this type and celebrates with a big party in the winery for employees, family, and friends. When the convoy of shipping trucks departs at midnight, it gets a police escort and enthusiastic cheering from the revelers. Distributors, working overtime, ship it worldwide in a matter of hours.

- 8 shallots, peeled and sliced
- 2 tablespoons olive oil
- 4 sausages (authentic French garlic sausages, *saucisson*, are available in gourmet shops)
- ½ cup Beaujolais

Heat oven to 375°F. Sauté shallots in hot olive oil in sauté pan. Add wine when shallots are translucent. Pierce sausages with a fork and place in a baking dish just large enough to hold them. Top with wine-shallot mixture. Bake for 20 to 25 minutes, until heated thoroughly. Serve with French bread.

Nathalie Longefay's Potatoes au Gratin

SERVES 4

This simple dish is the one Nathalie most missed from home. What does she miss most now that she lives back in France? Chips and salsa!

- 2 pounds russet potatoes
- 2 tablespoons butter, divided into 1-tablespoon pieces
- 4 ounces Gruyère cheese, grated
- 2 cloves garlic, minced
  salt and pepper to taste
- 3 cups boiled milk (or half milk and half cream)

Preheat oven to 350°F. Peel and slice the potatoes thin. Butter a casserole with 1 tablespoon butter and arrange a layer of potato slices in it. Top with half the grated cheese and the garlic, and season with salt and pepper. Arrange the rest of the potato slices and top with the rest of the cheese. Season and dot the top with the remaining butter cut into bits. Pour the hot milk over all. Bake for 40 to 60 minutes, or until top is well browned and all the liquid has been absorbed.

Tip

Denise Longefay cooks the potato mixture on top of the stove in a heavy casserole before finishing it in the oven.

Cultural Heritage Festival activities and food draw folks to the Boal Mansion.

Festivals that celebrate cultural diversity are popular in Central Pennsylvania, where cultures have been blending for generations. The Boal Mansion in Boalsburg, which hosted a Cultural Heritage Festival for several years, is a still-evolving example of the process. At the Columbus Chapel and Boal Mansion Museum, visitors can see heirlooms dating from the fifteenth century in the Columbus family's private chapel from Spain, as well as the mansion's original eighteenth-century furnishings.

Chris Lee, an eighth-generation Boal and owner of the mansion, commented about his daughter Susanna: "Just look at her. She's 50 percent German, and I don't even have one drop of German blood." Lee does have almost every other Western European country represented in his lineage—French, Scottish, Irish, English, and Spanish. Susanna's mother, the former Jennie Yost, supplied the German ancestry.

Grandma Elizabeth Yost's German Raw Apple Cake

SERVES 12

Jennie Lee provided her grandmother's recipe for an easy fresh apple cake offered at the Cultural Heritage Festival that took place on the Boal Mansion grounds in 1989. Pennsylvania Dutch and delicious, the cake is an old-fashioned favorite.

1¾ cups granulated sugar

3 eggs

1 cup vegetable oil

2 cups flour

1 teaspoon baking soda

1 teaspoon cinnamon

¼ teaspoon salt

1 cup chopped nuts

2 cups chopped, pared apples

Preheat oven to 350°F. Beat together sugar, eggs, and oil until blended. Combine flour, baking soda, cinnamon, and salt and add to the wet ingredients. Fold in nuts and apples. Spray a 9 x 13 inch baking pan with nonstick cooking spray or grease and pour in the batter. Bake for 45 minutes, or until toothpick inserted near the center comes out clean. Cool and dust with confectioner's sugar or serve warm with ice cream. This cake keeps for days and seems to improve as it gets older.

Cook's Note

A nonfat, lower-calorie version could also be made by reducing the sugar to 1 cup, by replacing the 1 cup of oil with 1 cup of applesauce, and by eliminating the nuts. Many tasters preferred the nonfat version to the original. Both are delicious.

Tip

Lay a paper doily on top of the cake and sprinkle with powdered sugar. Remove doily and enjoy the lacy effect.

Thanksgiving

The Thanksgiving holiday is generally a quiet time in the Centre Region. People gather in family groups to mark the passing of another year and to count their blessings. Downtown State College is deserted on Thanksgiving Day, since students are, for the most part, home for the holiday. Some students live too far away and even might never have heard of Thanksgiving. These people are likely to head for Ye Old College Diner, where a 50-cent Thanksgiving dinner special makes individuals family.

The Diner serves about 1,500 people on Thanksgiving Day and donates the profits to charity. The menu is always the same—turkey, stuffing, gravy, mashed potatoes, cranberry sauce—and provides the flavors of the American holiday to those who might not otherwise get a chance to savor it.

Turkey Gravy

MAKES 2 CUPS

4 tablespoons fat from
turkey pan drippings

4 tablespoons flour

salt and pepper

2 cups turkey stock

After removing turkey from pan to a cutting board, pour liquid from pan into a liquid measure. Skim off the fat, reserving 4 tablespoons (or adding melted butter to equal 4 tablespoons). Place roasting pan over a burner on the stove and add the reserved fat. Use a whisk to scrape up all the browned drippings. Stir in the flour and blend well over medium heat for 3 minutes or until lightly browned. Season with salt and pepper to taste and slowly pour in the turkey stock, whisking constantly, until the mixture is smooth. Simmer for 10 minutes, then taste and adjust the seasoning.

Cook's Note

Use the neck and giblets from the turkey to make the stock for the gravy, but don't use the liver, because its taste is too strong for a stock.

Roast Turkey with Bread Stuffing

SERVES 12

1 12-pound turkey
bread stuffing
¼ pound butter
salt and pepper

Preheat oven to 325°F. Rinse turkey and pat it dry. Stuff body and neck cavity with Savory Bread Stuffing. Soften 4 tablespoons butter and rub on surface of turkey. Sprinkle with salt and pepper and place breast-side down, on parchment paper, on a V-shaped roasting rack in a roasting pan and put in oven. Melt remaining butter with ¼ cup water and use this liquid to baste the turkey every 15 minutes until enough juices have accumulated in the pan for basting. Cook for 15 minutes per pound if the turkey weighs less than 16 pounds, and 12 minutes per pound if turkey is heavier. Continue to baste every 20 minutes during cooking. Turn turkey breast-side up after 1 hour. Turkey is done when meat thermometer inserted in the thigh reaches 180°F, the temperature in the breast is 170°F, and in the stuffing is at 165°F. Allow to stand, tented with foil, for 20 minutes before removing all the stuffing and before carving.

Savory Bread Stuffing

MAKES 9 CUPS (ALLOW ¾ CUP STUFFING PER POUND OF TURKEY)

½ pound butter
½ cup finely chopped onion
½ cup finely chopped celery
10 cups dry bread cubes
2 tablespoons fresh sage, chopped
1 tablespoon fresh thyme
1 tablespoon fresh marjoram
salt and pepper to taste

Melt butter in skillet and stir in the onion and celery. Cook over low heat until onion is soft. Add this mixture to the bread cubes along with the herbs and salt and pepper.

Tip

An instant-read thermometer is essential in the kitchen. Unlike the old-fashioned type that remains in the product during cooking, these are used frequently during cooking time to insert into the product to get a quick and accurate reading.

Cook's Note

Locally raised fresh turkeys are widely available in our area and are well worth seeking out and ordering for a special Thanksgiving treat.

Hunter's Reward

Phil Sollman hunts and cooks on his land near Fillmore.

The home of Phil and Jeanne Sollman, outside Fillmore, is a private, idyllic environment wrested from the very earth by two careful and creative people. Phil is a craftsman and woodworker who uses the wealth of Pennsylvania to create a harmonious life in tune with the rhythms of the season and the land. In late fall, that means he participates in the harvest of the woods by hunting a deer that will provide all the red meat he and his wife Jeanne will consume in a year.

Thousands of hunters are in the woods in Central Pennsylvania for the first day of buck season, but few have the luxury of hunting in their own backyard. Phil realizes his good fortune. "I enjoy sitting in the tree stand in the early hours, being fully aware of all that is going on around me. But when I get cold I can go in for coffee."

The Sollmans have owned their eleven acres since 1976 and started building in 1979. Their home is a reflection of their conjoined artistry—Jeanne is a renowned sculptor and award-wining medalist—and the dwelling itself is a work of art. Phil has hewn the lumber himself and matched it with solid local stone in a fusion of the elements that complements the environment. The house, situated on a southern slope, has large windows that allow passive solar heat to warm the structure. A woodstove in the great room burns about one cord of wood a year, providing supplementary heat in the evenings and on cloudy days.

Both are venison enthusiasts who have their own technique for dealing with animals that Phil harvests. "The meat must be treated properly," said Jeanne. "It must hang for ten to fourteen days, depending on the weather, so the enzymatic processes that soften the tissue can occur. When an animal is hunted, especially if it is wounded and does not die instantly, there is adrenaline in the meat, which does not taste good. People who say they don't like venison probably had some that wasn't handled properly."

Phil likes to hunt because he likes to take advantage of the gifts at his doorstep and because hunting makes him feel he has some control over his life. The fact that he also likes to cook what he brings home makes Jeanne appreciative: "There is not a day that goes by that we don't realize how lucky we are."

Phil Sollman's
Moroccan Tagine of Venison

SERVES 6

2 pounds venison shoulder,
  cut into 1½-inch chunks

7 tablespoons olive oil, divided

  pinch of saffron

1 cinnamon stick

1 large onion, peeled and finely chopped

¼ teaspoon freshly ground pepper

  salt

1½ cups dry red wine

½ cup blanched almonds

½ teaspoon ground cinnamon

½ pound dried dates

1 tablespoon sesame seeds

Put the meat in a pan with 6 tablespoons olive oil, saffron, cinnamon stick, onion, pepper, and salt. Pour on the red wine to barely cover the meat. Put a tight-fitting lid on the pan and bring to a boil, then reduce the heat and simmer gently for 1 to 1½ hours, stirring occasionally. Add additional wine or water as needed.

Heat 1 tablespoon olive oil and fry the almonds until golden brown, drain on paper towels, and set aside. Toast the sesame seeds in a moderate oven (350°F) until golden brown and set aside. Add the ground cinnamon to the meat and continue to cook, covered, for an additional 20 to 30 minutes, or until the meat is very tender.

Remove the meat from the pan with a slotted spoon and place it in an ovenproof serving dish. Keep warm, loosely covered with foil, in a very low oven. Add the dates to the sauce in the pan and cook gently for 10 to 12 minutes. Spoon dates and sauce over the meat. Scatter the almonds and sesame seeds over the top and serve.

Cook's Note

The word "venison" comes from the Latin "venir," to hunt, and relates to the meat of all species of deer. Venison is very lean, and overcooking tends to make it livery-tasting. Steaks and tender cuts like the tenderloin are best cooked rare or medium rare. Tougher cuts, like the leg or shoulder, benefit from marinating and slow-cooking, especially with an acid ingredient like wine or cider.

Warning

Women who are pregnant, or people with weakened immune systems, should not eat venison, or other meat, when it is raw or undercooked.

Venison Tenderloin Diablo

SERVES 4

1 pound tenderloin of venison

1 cup dry red wine

2 tablespoons Dijon mustard

2 tablespoons cracked black pepper

1 tablespoon oil

1 to 2 tablespoons butter

Marinate venison loin in red wine for an hour or so, then pour off the wine and reserve. Spread the meat with the mustard and roll in the peppercorns to coat. Sauté the coated loin in hot oil until rare, about 10 minutes. Remove from the heat, pour in wine marinade, and reduce. Add butter one teaspoon at a time while whisking. Taste for seasoning and strain if necessary. Slice the loin, arrange on a warm serving platter, and pour the sauce on top.

Venison Steaks with Morel Sauce

SERVES 4

4 venison steaks or cutlets, 4 to 6 ounces each

1 cup dry red wine

1 tablespoon olive oil

2 tablespoons onion, minced

1 tablespoon garlic, minced

1 tablespoon red or green pepper, minced

1 cup morels, sliced if large

1 tablespoon flour

¼ cup stock: chicken, beef, or vegetable

2 tablespoons butter

1 tablespoon bacon fat

Marinate venison in red wine for about 1 hour. Heat olive oil and sauté onion, garlic, and pepper until tender. Coat morels with flour and add to the vegetables, sautéing until brown. Remove venison from the marinade and add the marinade to the pan with the morels along with the stock. Simmer. Stir in the butter, one teaspoon at a time. Heat bacon fat in separate sauté pan and, when hot, sear the steaks and cook rare. Top with the morel sauce.

Winter

Winter
Recipes

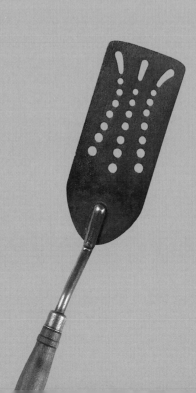

Winter

*P*reparations for the holiday season dominate December in Central Pennsylvania, and gradually the whole town cooperates and is transformed into a sparkling marvel. The baking season is in full swing, and cooks are busy rolling and cutting out cookies for the busy entertaining season. Decorations used once a year are lovingly unwrapped, eliciting floods of memories.

Those with a bent for architecture are constructing gingerbread houses and getting sticky fingers attaching gumdrops and candy canes. Bellefonte shines with an elegant glow during the Victorian Christmas celebration that shows off the extraordinary dwellings that lend an air of character to the scenic town.

With the closing of Penn State after the busy fall semester, the students empty out and it's possible to get parking on the street once again. Permanent residents emerge and meet each other in State College and the surrounding towns to do holiday shopping. The solstice on December 21 marks the least amount of daylight, and the year closes in on itself. It's dark when you go to work and dark when you scurry home, eager to find consolation in a warming bowl of venison chili or chicken soup.

Our religious observances bring forth the light. Hanukkah and Kwanza are both candle-lighting holidays, and wherever Christmas is celebrated a decorated evergreen tree shines brightly. The holiday time is marked with religious observances—families attend services together, joyous music rocks the vaulted ceilings in churches, choirs bringing heavenly song to congregations large and small all over the area.

The week between Christmas and New Year's is a festive one, with rounds of holiday parties often overlapping. By New Year's Eve, the partying reaches a crescendo and the celebrators ring in the New Year loud and clear. Restaurants and hotels are packed to capacity with revelers, and parties among friends are increasingly popular with those old enough to have already gone out a few times on New Year's Eve. The First Night celebration in downtown State College offers a variety of family-oriented events, and the ice sculptures make venturing into town worthwhile no matter how bad the weather is.

New Year's Day is often an occasion to eat special foods to guarantee good fortune in the coming year. Many ethnic traditions appear at this time. Pork and sauerkraut? Hoppin' John? Why not both? Tomorrow you can diet!

January is the quietest time in the region—unless you are a skier. In that case, Tussey Mountain Ski Area puts an alpine-like experience at your doorstep. Minutes from State College, the resort starts making snow as soon as the weather is cold enough. I'm not an adventurous skier, but the trip up the chairlift at least once a year to see the view of the valley from the top is worth any number of falls it takes to get back down again.

Ice-skating at Stone Valley or another frozen lake is an outdoor experience in the Centre Region not to be missed. The feel of the irregular surface when skating on a lake adds a more challenging dimension to the sport. Ice-fishing at area lakes is also popular with the more hardy anglers.

Martin Luther King Day relieves some of the tedium of the dark days of winter, but most of

January is marked by shivering through frigid mornings, scraping car windows to remove layers of ice, and trying to keep the sidewalks clear. There is always the hope when you go to bed at night, though, that just maybe you will wake up to enough snow that work and school will be called off. Then snowmen sprout on the lawns, and snowball fights wreak havoc on campus.

Respite from the weather comes from home and hearth during these dark days of winter. Friends gather for gourmet dinner club "meetings," and an invitation to tea can heal a soul sick of the elements. Just when you think you can't bear it anymore, it's Groundhog Day, that singular Pennsylvania festival that has the eyes of the world focused on a sleeping woodchuck. Now we can blame the rest of the bad weather on this scapegoat. Whether he's wrong or right, one thing is certain: spring is only six weeks away.

Now life is hushed in the forest, crystal
blanket traps warmth from below
Penn's Woods resplendent in contrast
to billows of white drifted snow.

Bonnie Leedy's Cutout Cookies

MAKES ABOUT 6 DOZEN

Bonnie Leedy of State College is a professional baker with a home baking business, Bonnie's Desserts, that gives her the freedom to stay at home with her three children. Specializing in cookies, she also makes muffins for the Cheese Shoppe, and wedding and special-occasion cakes. Fascinated with baking since high school, Bonnie took cake-decorating lessons from a friend and truly enjoys the art. Her favorite cookie is chocolate chip, but she is always trying new recipes and likes to experiment with ethnic cookies like Puerto Rican Almond Tile Cookies or Italian Florentines. Bonnie's husband, John, is manager of The Tavern Restaurant and is always a willing tester for her baking experiments.

1 cup butter, softened

2 cups sugar

2 eggs, well beaten

1 teaspoon vanilla

½ cup milk

3¾ cups flour

½ teaspoon baking soda

Creamy Decorator Icing

Cream together butter, sugar, and eggs. Add remaining ingredients and mix until well blended. Refrigerate mixture up to 4 hours or freeze for 10 days. Allow dough to come to room temperature before rolling and cutting.

Roll ¼ inch thick on a well-floured pastry cloth. Cut into desired shapes with cookie cutter. Place on greased (or parchment-lined) baking sheets and sprinkle with sugar if desired. Bake at 375°F for 8 to 10 minutes, or until lightly browned. Remove from the oven and allow cookies to cool for a minute before removing to wire racks to cool completely. Decorate as desired with Creamy Decorator Icing.

Creamy Decorator Icing

Blend 1½ cups sifted confectioners' sugar with ¼ teaspoon vanilla and enough heavy cream to make the icing easy to spread or pipe onto cookies. Color with food coloring if desired.

Holiday Preparations

Catherine Lee and Virginia Dale Ricker pour coffee at a holiday party. Granddaughter Rebecca Dale Ricker-Gilbert samples a doughnut.

One of the local traditions that inaugurated the holiday season in the Centre Region for years was the annual Christmas Coffee held by Virginia Dale Ricker in early December. Named "Mrs. Hospitality" by Town & Gown, *Mrs. Ricker was assisted by her cousin Catherine Lee, whose late husband, J. Marvin Lee, wrote "Centre County: The County in Which We Live."*

For more than two decades, the circular driveway in front of Woodsdale, the Ricker home, was the artery that delivered scores of women who chatted their way through the garlands on the front door. Once inside, the aroma of coffee, cinnamon, and fresh pine welcomed guests to the distinctive Pennsylvania farmhouse.

In a town with a constantly changing population, traditions are sometimes difficult to establish. Not so in the Ricker circle of friends—which encompassed daughter Heather Ricker-Gilbert's contemporaries as well as her mother's. What began as a neighborhood party came to include women from all around the area.

For years Mrs. Lee tantalized onlookers by frying homemade doughnuts at the dining room table and providing plates of various toppings—powdered sugar, cinnamon sugar, coconut, chocolate—that enabled guests to participate in the final assembly. The arrangement also ensured that each person would try more than one, for comparison. Although in later years the menus were simplified to a variety of coffee-cakes, the coffee itself remained a highlight. Poured from a silver coffeepot into china cups, the coffee could be topped with shaved chocolate or whipped cream, or fortified by adding some Irish whiskey or bourbon from discreet old-fashioned flowered pitchers.

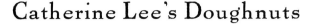

Catherine Lee's Doughnuts

MAKES 6 DOZEN

This recipe has been used in Centre County for about a hundred years. Grandma Schreck of Lemont gave it to Catherine Lee in 1934, when Catherine was a bride. Mrs. Lee used to triple it to feed 150 ladies at the Christmas Coffee. It was previously published in a cookbook co-authored by Heather Ricker-Gilbert and Nancy Spear, Cooking Around the College, *published in 1981 by Oxon Press of State College.*

2 eggs	4 tablespoons baking powder
4 cups white sugar	
4 cups sweet milk	4 teaspoons salt
8 tablespoons butter, melted	oil for deep-frying
10 to 12 cups flour	optional toppings: powdered sugar, cinnamon sugar, coconut, chocolate
1 tablespoon nutmeg	

Beat the eggs and slowly add the sugar, beating all the while. Stir in the milk and butter. Mix 10 cups of the flour with the nutmeg, baking powder, and salt. Mix the dry and the moist ingredients together, adding additional flour if necessary to keep the mixture just firm enough to handle. Chill the dough and roll to ½-inch thickness. Cut with a large doughnut cutter. Fry in oil heated to 350° to 375°F until golden brown on both sides, about 3 minutes. Using an electric skillet for frying doughnuts gives a wide surface area and an even heat. Set the thermostat for 365°F and adjust up or down as needed. The doughnuts should be turned over only one time or they will absorb too much of the oil.

Virginia Ricker's Bishop's Bread

SERVES 12

2½ cups all-purpose flour
½ teaspoon salt
1 teaspoon cinnamon
½ cup butter
2 cups brown sugar
1 teaspoon baking powder
½ teaspoon baking soda
1 egg, beaten
¾ cup sour milk or buttermilk

Preheat oven to 350°F. Grease or spray two 8-inch cake pans. Stir flour, salt, and cinnamon together and cut in butter. Save ¾ of this mixture for the top crumbs. To the remaining dry mix add baking powder and baking soda and stir together. Combine beaten egg and sour milk or buttermilk and add to the dry mix, beating briskly. Pour into prepared pans and scatter the crumbs on the top. Bake for 25 minutes until cakes test done with a toothpick. One cup nuts or raisins, or additional cinnamon, may be added to the batter.

Author's Note

The glowing embers of tradition were fanned in the Ricker household at those Christmas Coffees. As I moved throughout the home, looking at the many old photographs of the family and the region, I connected with the people who were here before, whose names streets and parks and summits bear. I connected with Christian Dale, an early settler of Centre County, as I stepped out of the home and looked over at Mount Nittany. By opening her home and her heart, Mrs. Ricker gave the gift of tradition to her many friends and helped to make us all one, all residents of Centre County.

Sally Kennedy decorates her gingerbread house.

Bellefonte's Victorian Christmas celebration is an annual event that showcases the splendor of a bygone age during a festive weekend in mid-December. Events kick off Friday night with holiday music and a candle-lighting ceremony on the steps of the county courthouse perched high on the square (except in Bellefonte it's called a diamond) with a panoramic view of the picturesque town. Throughout the weekend there are home tours, concerts, train excursions, horse-and-carriage rides, an arts and crafts fair, a model railroad display, tea parties for young and old, and a gingerbread house contest. Entries for the gingerbread house contest decorate the windows of the Diamond Deli, eliciting ohs and ahs from impressed passersby.

Before I met Sally Kennedy, I was never drawn to the holiday medium of gingerbread houses; they seemed too childish, too saccharine—all that candy, all that gooey icing. Since meeting Sally, though, and since smelling that lingering ginger aroma in her home, I have acquired an abiding appreciation for this art form. Just as when you replace a front door or build your first deck or construct a stone wall, your vision narrows once you are entrenched in a project. All you can see are front doors, or decks, or stone walls. Confronting something for the first time encourages a myopic view of the universe.

Sally described her own initial involvement. "I just wanted to do a fun holiday project with my granddaughter Lisa. I was very surprised when it took first place in the contest." Sally, who works part-time as a medical technician at Penn State, fit the project into her schedule. "You need to make the dough ahead and then chill it," she said. "Construct the walls and let them set. It really is better to do a little bit each day." The entire structure took about a week to complete, with approximately eight actual hands-on hours.

Now she gives workshops on the medium and encourages everyone to give it a try. "Oh, it's easy," she maintains. "I used the December 1996 issue of Bon Appetit *magazine, with its cooking-class article titled 'Building the Perfect Gingerbread House' for my inspiration. The directions are clear, and there are even step-by-step photos."*

Even if your gingerbread house is lopsided, your kitchen will still smell wonderful, and you really will have visions of sugarplums dancing in your head.

Foolproof Gingerbread Dough

MAKES ENOUGH FOR ONE HOUSE OR 6 DOZEN CUTOUT COOKIES

This recipe for gingerbread dough came from my sister-in-law, Barbra Quinn. As its name implies, it is very easy to roll out. I have used this recipe for cooking demonstrations at area schools, and the children were all able to roll out and cut their own creations. Using a blackstrap molasses gives a rich, dark sheen to the dough and to the finished product.

1 cup blackstrap molasses

1 cup brown sugar

1 tablespoon powdered ginger

¾ teaspoon cinnamon

⅜ teaspoon cloves

1 tablespoon baking soda

1 cup butter

2 eggs

7½ cups flour

Preheat oven to 325°F. Heat molasses, brown sugar, ginger, cinnamon, and cloves to the boiling point. Remove from the heat and add the baking soda. Pour the hot mixture over the butter in a large, deep mixing bowl (use a heavy-duty mixer if available). Stir slowly with dough hook until butter is melted. Add the eggs and the flour alternately and knead until smooth. Roll and cut out with cookie cutters or by using templates as a guide. Bake on parchment-lined cookie sheets for 8 to 10 minutes.

Icing for Gingerbread

4 large egg whites

7 cups powdered sugar
(approximately 2 pounds)

In the deep bowl of a heavy-duty mixer, beat the egg whites until very foamy. Add powdered sugar ½ cup at time. Beat until well blended after each addition and scrape down the sides of the bowl. When all the powdered sugar has been incorporated, beat the icing at high speed until very thick and glossy, about 5 minutes.

Sally Kennedy's Tips for Gingerbread House Builders

Roll the dough between two sheets of parchment paper.

Use ¼-inch guides to roll out the dough.

Cut the dough with a pizza cutter.

Smaller pieces of dough do not take as long to bake as the larger ones.

Use meringue powder for the icing, to avoid the risk of salmonella from raw egg white.

Use a heavy-duty mixer to get the icing really smooth and glossy.

Use small pastry bags to pipe the icing, because it quickly gets as hard as concrete.

Decorate the inside of the house before putting on the roof.

Gifts from the Kitchen

The holiday season in Central Pennsylvania is an exciting time when parties and open houses brighten neighborhoods throughout the month of December. Often, guests bring along hostess gifts, which are even more special when they are homemade. You can tell who is entertaining by the number of cars parked on the street.

Rosemary Walnuts

MAKES 4 CUPS

- 1 pound walnut halves
- 2 tablespoons clarified butter
- 2 tablespoons olive oil
- 5 tablespoons finely chopped fresh rosemary or 1½ tablespoons dried rosemary
- 1 teaspoon paprika
- 2 teaspoons kosher salt

Preheat oven to 325°F. Spread the walnuts in a single layer on a large baking sheet. Combine the clarified butter and olive oil, drizzle over the nuts, and stir to coat. Scatter the rosemary, paprika, and salt evenly over the nuts. Bake for 20 to 25 minutes, stirring with a metal spatula and shaking the pan so the nuts are evenly toasted. When they are golden brown they are ready. Allow to cool completely and store in an airtight container.

Curried Cashews

MAKES 6 CUPS

My husband, John, finds these irresistible. When I make them, I hide them in a yogurt container in the rear of the pantry and label them "Bread Crumbs" or some other unappealing name, so he is not tempted.

- 1½ pounds raw cashews
- 6 tablespoons clarified butter
- 1 tablespoon curry powder
- 2 teaspoons cumin
- 1 scant teaspoon kosher salt

Preheat oven to 325°F. Toss the cashews with the clarified butter and spread them on a baking sheet. Roast the nuts for about 20 minutes, stirring often to ensure even browning. Mix the curry powder, cumin, and salt. When the cashews are golden brown, sprinkle them with the spices and allow the nuts to cool. Hide them.

Raspberry Truffles

MAKES ABOUT 40

- ½ cup heavy cream
- 12 ounces best-quality semisweet chocolate, chopped fine
- ¼ cup unsalted butter, cut into bits
- ½ cup seedless raspberry jam
- 2 tablespoons Chambord or other raspberry liqueur
- ½ cup cocoa powder for coating the truffles

Heat the cream over medium-low heat and add the chocolate when it is hot. Remove from the heat and stir with a whisk to melt the chocolate into the cream. Add the butter, whisking to incorporate a little at a time. Whisk in the jam and the Chambord, then transfer the mixture to a shallow cake pan. Chill in refrigerator, covered, for 4 hours, or until firm enough to shape. When firm enough to shape, place the cocoa powder into another cake pan. Make tiny round shapes using two teaspoons or a small scoop and roll in the cocoa powder to cover. Chill the truffles on a waxed-paper-lined baking tray and transfer to airtight container for longer storage.

Toasted Coconut Rum Truffles

MAKES ABOUT 40

- 2⅔ cups flaked coconut
- 12 ounces best-quality semisweet chocolate, chopped
- ½ cup heavy cream
- ¼ cup unsalted butter, cut into small bits
- ¼ cup dark rum

Preheat oven to 375°F. Toast the coconut on a baking sheet until golden brown, about 15 minutes, stirring frequently. Let cool. Combine the chocolate, butter, cream, rum, and 1 cup of the toasted coconut and heat in a heavy-bottom medium saucepan over moderate heat until smooth, whisking constantly. Transfer the mixture to a cake pan and chill, covered, for 4 hours, or until firm. When firm enough to shape, place the remaining toasted coconut in another cake pan. Make tiny round shapes using two teaspoons or a small scoop, then roll in toasted coconut to cover. Chill the truffles on a waxed-paper-lined baking tray, then transfer later to an airtight container for longer storage.

Tip

Using a tiny spring-release scoop available at a kitchenware or restaurant equipment store helps the truffle-rolling go much faster. With the scoop, the gooey chocolate mixture can be tapped against the edge of the cake pan so it drops into the coating mixture.

Patty Mitchell (above) recalls homesteading relatives of Central Pennsylvania: her great-great-aunt Bertha (near left) and her great-grandmother Nette (far left).

A landmark coming-of-age is noted when the family traditions are taken up by the next generation. Which of the children become the keepers? The ones that keep the outside world at bay by drawing the loved ones closer through aural, visual, and gustatory cues that encircle them like a cocoon. As families multiply and disperse, it is curious to note what they carry with them. What traditions from the Old Country are preserved in the offspring of those who made that great wrenching move from the homeland?

For Patty Mitchell's family, it is their Hutzlie Bread, or "Hutzel Brod," a nearly 100-year-old family recipe from Germany: "Sabina Roesch, my great-great-grandmother, brought a recipe from Germany, and her daughters Anntoinette and Bertha adapted it through the years according to the preferences of in-laws and siblings. Nette taught my grandmother, Honey, who taught my mother, Shirley. Nette and Honey would make their bread at Christmas and store it in the root cellar for as long as it lasted; they practically competed with each other to see who could keep the last loaf. I remember hearing that one of them had a loaf at Easter!"

Patty became a keeper in 1998 when she made the bread for the first time. She took up the family torch and uses it to warm her own heart and the hearts of family and friends that share the communion of the Hutzlie Bread.

Patty Mitchell's Hutzlie Bread *(Hutzel Brod)*

MAKES 6 LARGE LOAVES OR 15 TO 18 SMALL GIFT LOAVES

1 pound prunes

5 ounces golden raisins

5 ounces currants

8 ounces dried figs

4 ounces dried apricots

6 ounces cranberries

1 cup cream sherry

grated rind and juice
of 1 orange

2 large tart apples

1 cup chopped nuts

⅔ cup sugar

2 cakes yeast

½ cup warm water (110°F)

6 cups unbleached
white flour

1 stick butter
(not margarine)

2 eggs, slightly beaten

1 teaspoon cinnamon

½ teaspoon cloves

1 teaspoon anise seed

½ teaspoon cardamom
powder

2 teaspoons salt

Prepare the fruit mixture the night before: Stew the prunes in enough water to cover and set aside. Chop and mix all the remaining dried fruits with the whole cranberries; add the sherry, orange juice, and orange rind. Cover with plastic wrap and set aside overnight.

Early the next morning: Peel and chop the apples; add to the fruit and sherry mixture along with the nuts. Heat the prunes slightly (no higher than 110°F) and add the sugar to them, stirring to dissolve. Soften the yeast in the warm water in a large bowl, then add the warm prune-sugar mixture. Add 2 cups of flour and stir. Wait until the sponge rises (20 to 40 minutes). Melt the butter and incorporate it into the sponge. Add the 2 beaten eggs and mix. Mix the spices and salt into the remaining 4 cups of flour. Add 2 cups of the flour mixture to the sponge. Add half the fruit mixture and mix into the dough. Add the remaining flour and mix it in, then add the rest of the fruit-nut mixture.

Turn the dough out onto a floured tabletop or countertop. Add a little more flour as you knead to make a soft dough (at least 10 minutes). The prunes and some of the other fruit will break up during this manipulation. When it is ready, set the dough in a large, buttered bowl. Cover and let rise until doubled. Punch down the dough and turn out onto the floured work surface. Divide into loaves, kneading each a little and shaping. Place in buttered loaf pans. Cover pans and let rise for 1 hour.

Fifteen minutes before baking time, preheat oven to 350°F. Place the loaves in the oven and bake until done (about 25 to 30 minutes for small loaves and 45 to 50 minutes for large loaves). The loaf should sound hollow when tapped on the bottom. Remove bread from the pans and let cool on wire racks.

Tips

When working with many small loaves, put the loaf pans on a large baking sheet in order to move them in and out of the oven easily.

When using both racks of the oven, protect the loaves on the bottom shelf by placing them on two baking sheets. This will help prevent the bottoms from getting too dark.

Cook's Note

This bread does get a little dry if you store it at room temperature for more than a week (if it lasts that long), so eating it with butter is advised. Of course, we can freeze the bread now.

Polish Christmas Eve

By December 24, everyone who celebrates Christmas is at home engrossed in preparations. The mall is closed, the shops downtown are quiet, and even the crowd at the Allen Street Grill has dissipated. Everyone who can heads to home and hearth.

Holidays take us back to our roots. We seek the aromas, flavors, sounds, and sights of our child-hood and try to explore the family tree. Traditions that may have been lost for a generation resurface as we try to connect with who we are and whence we came. Fortunate are those who remember.

Neighbors Marty Mazur and Stan Giner are two of those fortunate ones. Both of Polish descent, they celebrate the Christmas traditions of their ancestors in time-honored ways by holding fast to the Wigilia (ve-geel-ya, with a hard "g"), or Christmas Eve supper, one of the most important meals of the year for Polish people.

Elements of the Wigilia are ceremonial, the same way the Greek Easter dinner and the Passover feast are. Just as the Judaic tradition holds the clan together through repeated use of certain foods and shared memories, so does the Wigilia. Specific dishes are served, certain restrictions are obeyed. It is a ritual.

The enthusiasm and dedication of the Mazur-Giner Wigilia proves time and again that "Wszystkie stare czasy sa dobre"—"All times are good when old."

Marty and Vicky Mazur's Pierogi

MAKES ABOUT 7 DOZEN

A recipe handed down by Marty's Grandma Odziemiec.

6 cups sifted flour	3 whole eggs
1 teaspoon salt	½ pint sour cream
1 stick melted margarine	Pierogi Fillings
½ cup milk	

Sift flour and salt into bowl. Add melted margarine, milk, eggs, and sour cream. Mix to form dough that is easy to handle. Knead on a board for a few minutes. Take an egg-size piece of dough and roll it out on a floured board. Cut out a small (roughly 2 inches in diameter) circle using a cup or a biscuit cutter. Place 1 teaspoon of filling onto the circle. Dampen the edge of the circle with water and fold over. Seal with a fork or turnover press. Cook pierogi six at a time in a large kettle of boiling water. Boil for about 5 minutes. After cooling, freeze to store.

To serve, fry with butter and onions until the onions are caramelized and the pierogi are beginning to brown. Some people like to serve sour cream on the side.

Pierogi Fillings

Here are three fillings you can use for pierogi. There are many others, including mashed potato, potato and cheese, and mushroom duxelles. Experiment!

SAUERKRAUT FILLING:

- 6 dried mushrooms (Polish mushrooms, if possible)
- 1 tablespoon butter
- 1 onion, finely diced
- ½ teaspoon salt
- ½ teaspoon freshly ground pepper
- 1 one-pound bag of sauerkraut
- 2 teaspoons sugar

Hydrate the dried mushrooms by pouring boiling water over them just to cover. Allow to stand for 15 minutes. Melt the butter in a frying pan and sauté the onions until translucent. Remove mushrooms from the soaking liquid and chop them finely. Add to the sautéed onions, then season with salt and pepper. Add the sauerkraut and sugar and cook to combine the flavors.

FARMER'S CHEESE FILLING:

- 1 pound farmer's cheese (or ricotta)
- 3 tablespoons sugar
- 3 eggs

Mix ingredients, adding more sugar, if desired.

PRUNE FILLING:

Use one dried, pitted prune per pierogi.

Tip

Strain the mushroom-soaking liquid through cheesecloth or a coffee filter to remove any grit, then add this liquid to the frying pan. Cook to reduce and concentrate the mushroom flavor.

New Year's Eve

Michele Ebaugh toasts the New Year.

The eve of the New Year has a long-standing, worldwide tradition of merrymaking, and in Central Pennsylvania that holds true as well. New Year's Eve is a noisy time. Evil spirits that roam the earth are banished by the commotion made by sirens and horns and the banging of pots and pans. Even excessive drinking has roots in antiquity—it is left over from a rite originally devised to remind people of the chaotic world that existed before God put the world in order.

Each New Year's Eve since 1990, Michele and Walter Ebaugh have entertained a good number of merrymakers in their Redwood Lane home. "We invite all the neighbors, so there isn't really anyone who would complain," said Michele of the annual semi-outdoor event. The Ebaughs have a screened-in porch with a fireplace that boasts a blazing fire. In a circular dance, the guests that stay outdoors take turns moving from the edge of the flames to the cooler perimeters of the porch area. The champagne the guests bring stays plenty cold right on the porch table laden with champagne flutes, while the hors d'oeuvres the guests contribute are presented in the warmth of the house. Keeping it as simple as she can when entertaining fifty-plus people, each year Michele bakes a whole ham and makes a tasty mustard sauce to accompany it. Other standard dishes she provides are a refreshing grapefruit and avocado salad and a traditional Swiss fondue at midnight.

Michele Ebaugh's Mustard Sauce

MAKES ABOUT 4 CUPS

Few recipes are originals. Most have a history of being passed from one person to another in a chain that links us all. While I call this Michele Ebaugh's Mustard Sauce, she refers to it as Rae Chambers's Mustard Sauce, and the copy of the recipe that I have from Michele (who got it from Rae) reads "J.A.'s Mustard" and has written beneath it "from Eleanor Hempstead, at a Christmas party at Craig Claiborne's." In any case, it is a wonderful condiment to accompany the smoky flavors of the ham.

1   4-ounce can or two 2-ounce cans Coleman's dry mustard

1   cup tarragon vinegar

6   eggs

¾   cup sugar

¼   pound butter, cut into bits

1   teaspoon salt

Place mustard powder in the top portion of a nonreactive double boiler and pour the vinegar over it. Do not mix. Cover and allow to stand overnight, or at least 3 hours. After the standing time, place over simmering water and mix with a whisk until smooth. Add the eggs one at a time, whisking continually until thoroughly incorporated. Add the sugar and salt, and whisk the butter in one bit at a time, until the mixture is a smooth emulsion. The total cooking time should be about 5 minutes over a low heat. Do not overcook or the eggs will curdle. Put the mixture into individual jars and refrigerate. The mustard sauce will keep for months and is delicious with all meats and fish and on sandwiches.

Cook's Note

If the eggs are small, use an extra one.

Tip

If you use an aluminum pan for this you will end up with a gray, metallic mass as the aluminum reacts with the vinegar and mustard. Be sure to use stainless steel, enamel, or glass.

Michele Ebaugh's
Grapefruit and Avocado Salad

SERVES 12

Again, I credit this salad to Michele, but the recipe she gave me reads: "Mary Jane Fisher's Dressing for Grapefruit and Avocado Salad." Mary Jane Fisher is the mother of marine scientist Chuck Fisher, a neighbor who also attends the annual New Year's event. Chuck is an accomplished cook in his own right and tantalizes the neighborhood during the summer months with the aromas that emanate from his often-used grill.

Cook's Note

This very sweet dressing can be made with significantly less sugar, depending on how sweet you perceive grapefruit to be. Start with a couple of tablespoons and add more to your taste. This recipe makes a lot of dressing, but it keeps for several weeks in the refrigerator.

Tip

Section the grapefruit over a large bowl to collect the juices. Then, as you cut the avocado, gently coat each slice with the grapefruit juice to prevent discoloration.

DRESSING:

- 1½ cups sugar
- 2 teaspoons salt
- 2 teaspoons dry mustard
- 1 teaspoon paprika
- ⅔ cup cider vinegar
- 2 cups salad oil
- 1½ teaspoons celery seeds

Blend sugar, salt, mustard powder, and paprika. Slowly add the vinegar and salad oil, alternately, whisking well after each addition. Add the celery seeds and chill. Makes 3½ cups.

SALAD:

- 4 ruby-red grapefruit
- 4 avocados

Section the grapefruit. Arrange the sections on a large serving platter in a starburst pattern, leaving space between the sections to place the avocado. Peel and slice each avocado into four sections. Cut each quarter into three long slices. Nestle the avocado slices between the grapefruit sections and drizzle with the dressing. You will not need all the dressing for the one salad; store the remainder in the refrigerator.

New Year's Day

New Year's Day has long been a holiday, with roots that go back to prehistoric times. Ancient societies performed rites to abolish the past so people could start another cycle reborn in spirit. Today's "New Year's resolutions" are a continuation of that tradition of "turning over a new leaf."

Our holiday customs are linked to pagan year-end festivities in the Near East, northern Europe, and Rome. In 45 B.C., the Romans were the first to use January 1 as the beginning of the new year. Before then, the date of the vernal equinox, March 25, was considered the start of the new year.

The Jewish culture has its own eight-day Festival of Lights, Hanukkah, which helps to illuminate the dark days of winter. Africans and African Americans celebrate Kwanza for seven days with candles and the commemoration of seven basic principles. A New Year's Day tradition that has roots in an ancient fertility ritual from Africa is the Southern custom of eating black-eyed peas with hog jowl or ham, for "money in the pot" or good luck. In some areas of the South, the peas are combined with rice to make a traditional dish called "Hoppin' John."

Hoppin' John

(Black-Eyed Peas and Ham Hocks)

SERVES 8

For good luck throughout the year, serve the black-eyed peas over the rice.

- 2 1-pound ham hocks
- 2 cups (1 pound) dried black-eyed peas
- 1 cup coarsely chopped onions
- 1 cup chopped celery
- 1 fresh hot red chili pepper, or pepper flakes to taste
-    freshly ground black pepper
- 3 cups cooked white Carolina enriched rice

Place ham hocks in a heavy 5-quart pot and add enough water to cover the meat by at least 1 inch. Bring to a boil over high heat, reduce the heat to low, and simmer, partially covered, for 2 hours, or until the ham hocks are tender.

Sort and rinse the black-eyed peas. Add the peas, onion, celery, chili (or pepper flakes), and a few grindings of pepper to the pot. Mix well and bring to a boil over high heat. Reduce the heat to low, then simmer, partially covered, for 1 to 1½ hours, or until the peas are tender. Check the pot from time to time and add more water if necessary. When the peas are fully cooked they should have absorbed almost all the pan liquid. Serve over rice.

Cook's Note

Enriched rice should not be rinsed before cooking because the vitamins and minerals that are added would be washed off.

"Hair of the Dog" Pork and Sauerkraut

SERVES 10

Sometimes this is just what you need on New Year's Day. Serve this with Hoppin' John and cover all your good-luck bases.

10 boneless 1½-inch-thick pork cutlets

4 tablespoons safflower oil

1½ pounds kielbasa, cut into 2-inch lengths

1 large onion, sliced into crescent shapes

8 cloves garlic, chopped

2 cups Bloody Mary mix (see Cook's Note)

1½ ounces vodka

1½ ounces gin

½ cup brown sugar

2 quarts sauerkraut (Peachey's, in Barrville, makes good homemade sauerkraut)

Trim pork cutlets of visible fat and brown in hot safflower oil. As each is browned, remove it to a large casserole dish. Brown the kielbasa pieces and place in the casserole with the pork. Add the slivered onion and garlic to the pan drippings and cook until onion is translucent. Add Bloody Mary mix, vodka, and gin and simmer. Add brown sugar and stir to dissolve. Add the sauerkraut and cook to blend the flavors for 15 minutes.

Preheat oven to 275°F. Arrange the sauerkraut mixture over the pork and kielbasa in the casserole. Cover and bake for 4 hours. Check occasionally to be sure all the liquid has not evaporated. Water can be added if the mixture gets too dry.

Tip

This dish tastes much better when made at least one day ahead so the flavors have time to blend.

Cook's Note

Bloody Mary mix is easy to make by combining 3 cups of tomato juice with ¼ cup lemon juice and 2 tablespoons of Worcestershire sauce. Season to taste with salt, pepper, and hot-pepper sauce.

Martin Luther King Day

Mid-January marks the commemoration of Martin Luther King Day and gives the community an opportunity to evaluate the enduring contributions that African Americans have made to America. The term "soul food" relates to a cuisine that goes back to the roots of African Americans in the American South. Some of their favorite dishes were very simple foods, such as greens and parts of the pig not choice enough for the plantation masters. For many years blacks were detached from their culinary roots, but today there is an open acceptance and delight in this elemental and well-seasoned cuisine.

R.K., a State College resident and friend to both my sons, loves good food. Whenever he visits our house, he always gravitates to the kitchen or the grill to see what's cooking. Occasionally he calls with basic cooking questions, such as "I bought a chicken. What should I do with it?"

After his trip to Benin in 1998 with his mother and his father, who was on a Fulbright fellowship, R.K. brought his photos of Africa to our house. Almost every page of the photo album had pictures of tables of beautiful food surrounded by smiling people dressed in colorful clothing. Some of the shots were of the dusty village he visited, with eager children lining up for the photo; others were scenery shots of the jungle. When I first asked him how he liked his trip, he looked me straight in the eye and said, "I will never be the same."

Reconnecting with one's roots expands a sense of self. R.K.'s roots are diverse indeed and include his parents' roots in Rwanda, his own roots from his birthplace in Boston, and his childhood and adolescence in Central Pennsylvania. R.K., whose African name, is Rugigana Kavamahanga, which translates to "conqueror" and "lives abroad but will return," enjoys celebrating his African heritage. His fish and rice recipe was created from our conversations about dishes he enjoyed on his trip to Benin.

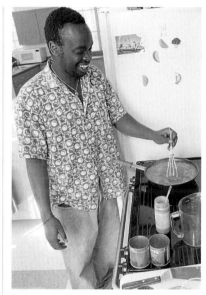

R.K.'s warm smile and a spicy dish heat up a January day.

R.K.'s Fish and Rice, Benin-Style

SERVES 6

1½ pounds boneless haddock fillets, with skin

2 tablespoons flour

salt and pepper

2 tablespoons oil

2 onions, chopped

2 cloves garlic, minced

1 teaspoon fresh ginger, grated

1 red and 1 green pepper, seeded and chopped

2 hot peppers, seeded and minced

2 teaspoons curry powder

16 ounces tomato sauce

2 ounces tomato paste

3 cups chicken or vegetable stock or water

2 cups long-grain rice

Rinse haddock fillets and pat dry. Combine flour, salt, and pepper. Pat skinless side of fish into flour mixture. Heat oil in large skillet until hot and place the haddock in the hot oil, with the skin on top, to lightly brown the fish on one side only. Remove and reserve the fish. To the oil remaining in the skillet add the onion, garlic, and ginger and sauté for 2 minutes, until the vegetables soften. Add the peppers and the hot peppers and cook for a few minutes, until the peppers start to soften. Add the curry powder, tomato sauce, and tomato paste and cook, stirring until well mixed. Add the stock or water and the rice and stir well. Cover the mixture and cook for 15 minutes. Place the reserved haddock fillets, with the skin side down, on top of the rice, cover the skillet, and cook for another 5 or 10 minutes, until the fish flakes easily with a fork and the rice is fully cooked. Remove the fish to a warm serving platter and serve the rice and vegetables in a large bowl.

Tip

You can streamline the production by omitting the flour and the initial browning of the fish. Just top the cooked rice and vegetable mixture with the seasoned raw fish fillets. Cover and cook for an additional 10 to 15 minutes, until the fish flakes easily.

Exotic Winter Produce

Central Pennsylvania may seem remote, but that does not stop us from getting the goods. Today it's much easier to satisfy a taste for sushi or Thai food—the ingredients are available at specialty markets. It has not always been so easy.

There have always been pioneers in the grocery arena, however. Temple Market on Beaver Avenue, which closed in the early 1970s, was one such venue. The grocery division at O. W. Houts has always carried a full complement of raw ingredients and gourmet items, thanks in large part to the efforts of Rose Quinn, who managed the department from 1965 to 1990.

Another influential person in the State College area has been Tom McKivison, produce manager for forty-one years at the Weis Market on Westerly Parkway in State College. Accommodating his many international customers was always his goal and, to that end, he had items shipped into Central Pennsylvania from all over the world.

In season, he stocked whatever was available locally. The rest of the year he was dependent on suppliers in New York and Baltimore. In an era when most of the other supermarkets carried only iceberg lettuce and pale imitators of true tomatoes in the winter, Tom McKivison brought in fresh ginger and cilantro, leeks, daikon, napa cabbage, mangoes, cherimoya, fennel, radicchio, celeriac, okra, and bitter melon.

Tom is now retired and volunteers at both the Boalsburg Museum and the Centre Furnace Mansion.

Tom McKivison displays exotic produce.

Stuffed Fennel

SERVES 4 TO 6

Cook's Note

In Central Pennsylvania grocery stores, the terms "fennel" and "anise" seem to be interchangeable. Although both are in the carrot family, Umbelliferae, *they are very different plants. Anise is* Pimpinella anisum, *an annual herb grown for its small, licorice-flavor seeds. Fennel is* Foeniculum vulgare, *a perennial or biennial herb with an appearance similar to celery but with a thickened, bulbous stem that is eaten raw or cooked. The seeds of fennel are also used for flavoring, such as in Italian sweet sausage, but they are larger than anise seeds. The most popular type of fennel is Florence fennel, called finnochio.*

4   fennel bulbs

6   tablespoons melted butter

2   cups fresh bread crumbs

2   eggs, beaten

½   cup chopped fresh parsley

2   cups tomato sauce

½   cup freshly grated Parmesan cheese

Cut the green upper stems and the feathery leaves from the fennel bulbs. Cut a slice from the bottom of each bulb to release its stalks and separate two or three of the stalks surrounding the closely closed heart. Reserve hearts for the stuffing. Parboil the fennel stalks for 5 minutes. Drain.

To prepare the stuffing, mince the reserved hearts and sauté them briefly in the butter. Add the bread crumbs, butter, eggs, and parsley. Fill each stalk and press the edges together. Arrange the stalks close together in a shallow, buttered casserole. Coat the filled fennel stalks with tomato sauce and sprinkle with the Parmesan. Bake at 350°F for about 40 minutes, or until browned on top.

Dinner Club

Residents of Central Pennsylvania with a yen for gourmet foods don't always need to travel to large cities to be satisfied. Some of them meet on their own to try various recipes. Cecil and Trudy Smith of State College are members of a dinner club that has been meeting, with some changes of participants, since 1982. Ray and Bobbi Lombra have been members since 1983, and Dick and Marie Fedon since 1988.

Cecil explained the parameters of the group. "The club is made up of three couples who get together every other month for a dinner that we take turns planning. The host invites a fourth couple to be guests. So far, we have never repeated a guest, and we don't intend to. That is one of the rules to keep the club interesting." Ray Lombra, associate dean of research and graduate studies in the College of the Liberal Arts at Penn State, talked about the key features of the club, which account for its success and longevity:

"The structure of the group is very important. First of all, the recipes chosen must have never been tried. This depersonalizes it and adds some suspense. We all feel free to criticize and make comments about a dish.

"Second, we get a lot of variety with the guest couple.

"Third, meeting every other month is just often enough. Each host gets to plan two dinners a year, during different seasons, which generally revolve around a certain theme."

Trudy Smith is the group's historian and has a thick file of all the menus used over the years. The following recipes are from Trudy's file and represent favorites of the group's dishes in each category.

Cecil and Trudy Smith set the table for Dinner Club guests.

Salmon and Scallop Roulades with Beurre Blanc

SERVES 4

The Dinner Club's best appetizer also makes a fine entrée.

- 1 1-pound boneless salmon fillet, cut from the thickest part of the fish
- ½ pound sea scallops
- 1 egg white
- 1 cup heavy cream
- salt and white pepper
- 2 tablespoons shallots, minced
- 2 tablespoons champagne vinegar
- scant ½ cup dry white wine
- Beurre Blanc

Preheat oven to 275°F. Butter a shallow casserole dish. Cut the salmon fillet in half at the widest part. Using a narrow fillet knife, cut each piece in half horizontally to end up with 4 thin slices of salmon fillet, about 4 ounces each. Puree the scallops in a food processor, then add egg white and blend for just a few seconds. Slowly drizzle in the cream until the mixture is well incorporated. Season the mixture with salt and white pepper.

Between two sheets of parchment paper, lightly pound the salmon to uniform thickness, taking care not to tear the delicate flesh. Divide the scallop mixture between the salmon pieces and, using the parchment paper to help, roll up the salmon pieces and place in the buttered baking dish. Sprinkle with the shallots, vinegar, white wine, and pepper. Bake the salmon rolls for 10 minutes, or until just done and the fish is opaque. Serve immediately with Beurre Blanc.

Beurre Blanc

- ¼ cup shallots, minced
- ¼ cup red-wine vinegar
- ¼ pound unsalted butter, softened
- ⅛ cup heavy cream

In a small, heavy saucepan, put the shallots and the vinegar and place over low heat. Cook and reduce until the liquid is evaporated. Whisk the butter in a small bit at a time until a smooth emulsion is formed. Add cream and warm gently for a minute.

Tip

Scallops have a small bit of connective tissue that used to anchor them into their shells. It should be removed before cooking because it is tough and chewy.

French Onion Soup

SERVES 8

The Dinner Club's best soup.

½ cup oil

6 large Spanish onions, coarsely chopped

1 sprig of fresh thyme

3 bay leaves

1 bottle dry red wine

10 cups beef stock

8 slices stale French bread

1 pound Gruyère cheese, grated

Heat oil in a large pot. Add onions and sauté until translucent. Add thyme sprig and bay leaves. Add the wine and heat for a few minutes over medium-high heat, so the wine reduces by one-third. Add the stock and cook uncovered for 20 minutes.

Pour the soup into eight large ovenproof bowls. Top each with a slice of French bread. Sprinkle each with the cheese, then flash under the broiler until the cheese melts and the top crust is golden. Serve at once.

Mixed Greens with Stilton Crouton

SERVES 8

The Dinner Club's best salad.

8 ounces crumbled Stilton cheese (can substitute blue cheese, or use Montrachet)

8 slices French bread (cut 1 inch thick on the diagonal)

24 ounces Mesclun salad mix (or substitute your own blend of Boston lettuce, baby endive, radicchio, and red leaf lettuce), cleaned, dried, and chilled

DRESSING:

⅔ cup walnut oil

4 tablespoons red-wine vinegar

2 teaspoons Dijon mustard

salt and pepper to taste

Preheat broiler. Spread cheese on the French bread slices and place on baking tray. Broil the cheese croutons until cheese is melted and bubbly, about 2 or 3 minutes. Watch carefully so the cheese does not burn. Combine dressing ingredients in a large bowl and whisk together. Add the greens and toss gently. Divide the greens on eight salad plates and top with a hot cheese crouton. Serve immediately.

Tip

Chill the salad plates by placing them in the refrigerator for 30 minutes before serving. The contrast of the cold greens and the hot cheese toast with this salad is especially appealing.

Tip (left recipe)

When peeling onions, just remove the outermost layer of onion along with the skin. Your peeling will go much faster and you can use the discarded part to make stock.

Woodsy Potato Gratin

SERVES 8

The Dinner Club's best vegetable.

1 ounce dried mushrooms (chanterelles, morels, cèpes, or any other variety)

1 cup boiling water

5 large russet potatoes

2 tablespoons butter, divided

3 cloves garlic, minced

2 cups milk

1 cup heavy cream

1 tablespoon parsley

1 tablespoon chives, chopped

1 teaspoon kosher salt

½ teaspoon white pepper

Place the dried mushrooms in a bowl and cover with the boiling water. Soak until the water is tepid, about 30 minutes. Strain the mushrooms through a coffee filter to remove grit and reserve the mushrooms. Boil the mushroom liquid in a small saucepan until it is reduced to ½ cup. Reserve liquid.

Preheat oven to 350°F. Butter a 2-quart shallow casserole with 1 tablespoon butter and set aside. Rinse the mushrooms and chop. Peel potatoes and slice thin. Heat remaining 1 tablespoon butter in a 5-quart saucepan and cook the chopped mushrooms and garlic for 2 minutes. Add the sliced potatoes, the reduced mushroom liquid, the milk, the cream, half the parsley, half the chives, and salt and pepper. Bring the mixture to a boil, stirring carefully. Transfer mixture to the prepared casserole dish and bake for about 1 hour, until the potatoes are tender. Garnish with the remaining parsley and chives at serving time.

Cook's Note

The Dinner Club would also serve a bright vegetable, such as carrots, with this menu. Just cook the carrots in water to barely cover with a bit of butter and a sprinkle of sugar and season with salt and pepper. Stir frequently and when the liquid is reduced, the carrots will be tender.

Barbecued Veal Chops

SERVES 4

The Dinner Club's best main course. Ray Lombra got this recipe from the New York Times Magazine, *July 12, 1987. The creator was New York City caterer and author Karen Lee, whose fifth book,* The Occasional Vegetarian, *was published by Warner Books in 1995.*

- 4 large veal loin chops, 1 ¼ inches thick, about ¾ pound each
- 1½ tablespoon dark soy sauce
- 2½ tablespoons olive oil
- 1½ tablespoons Spicy Mustard Sauce
- 1 tablespoon light rice miso
- 1½ tablespoons medium-dry sherry
- 1½ tablespoons minced ginger
- 2 cloves garlic, minced
- ⅓ cup scallions, in ⅛-inch rounds
- 1 tablespoon green peppercorns in brine, drained and crushed
- ½ teaspoon freshly ground black pepper

Trim the veal chops, removing most of the visible fat. Using a sharp knife, score the chops on both sides by making opposing diagonal slashes about ¼ inch deep. Combine the soy sauce, olive oil, Spicy Mustard Sauce, miso, sherry, ginger, garlic, scallions, peppercorns, and pepper in a bowl. Mix with whisk to thoroughly combine the mixture.

Place the chops in a nonreactive dish large enough to hold them in a single layer. Brush the marinade on both sides of the scored chops and allow to marinate for 12 hours in the refrigerator. Broil or grill the chops for 6 minutes on each side. When done, they should be pink on the inside and crusty on the outside.

Spicy Mustard Sauce

- 1 2-ounce tin Coleman's dry mustard
- ¾ cup dry sherry
- ½ cup Dijon mustard
- ½ cup Pommery whole-seed mustard

Use a whisk to beat the ingredients to a smooth emulsion. This mixture will keep indefinitely in the refrigerator. Makes 1¾ cups.

Cook's Note

Just double this recipe to make 8 servings if you are preparing for a larger group.

Milk Chocolate and Lemon Mousse Parfaits

SERVES 6

The Dinner Club's best dessert. Go ahead and dirty every bowl in your house while making this involved dessert. The results will be worth it.

MILK CHOCOLATE MOUSSE:

1¼ teaspoons unflavored gelatin

¼ cup cold water

5 ounces milk chocolate, chopped

2 tablespoons whipping cream

1 tablespoon unsweetened cocoa powder

2 egg yolks, room temperature

2 tablespoons sugar

1 teaspoon vanilla

pinch of salt

6 tablespoons chilled whipping cream

4 egg whites, room temperature

LEMON MOUSSE:

1¼ teaspoons unflavored gelatin

5 tablespoons fresh lemon juice

2 eggs, separated and at room temperature

⅓ cup sugar

¾ cup chilled whipping cream

GARNISH:

1 cup fresh raspberries

additional whipped cream for garnish, if desired

First, for the chocolate mousse, sprinkle 1¼ teaspoons unflavored gelatin over cold water in a small bowl. Let stand 10 minutes to soften. Set bowl in saucepan of simmering water and stir until dissolved.

In another small bowl set over a saucepan of simmering water, melt the chocolate with 2 tablespoons of cream and the cocoa, stirring with a small whisk until smooth. Add gelatin mixture to the chocolate mixture and stir until dissolved. With electric mixer, beat egg yolks, sugar, vanilla, and salt until thick and pale. Add chocolate mixture and beat briefly to combine. Transfer chocolate mixture to a large shallow bowl and cool.

Whip the 6 tablespoons of cream until soft peaks form. In another bowl, whip the egg whites until soft peaks form. Fold the egg-white mixture into the chocolate mixture, then gently fold in the whipped cream. Divide the chocolate mousse among six 10-ounce chilled wineglasses and refrigerate until set, about 1 hour.

For the lemon mousse, while the chocolate mousse is setting, sprinkle 1¼ teaspoons unflavored gelatin over the lemon juice in a small bowl. Let stand 10 minutes to soften. Beat yolks and sugar in medium metal bowl until thick and pale. Place the bowl over a saucepan of simmering water and stir until the sugar dissolves and the mixture thickens, about 5 minutes. Add the gelatin mixture and stir to dissolve. Refrigerate lemon mixture until just beginning to set, stirring frequently, about 20 minutes.

Whip the two egg whites and the ¾ cup cream in separate bowls until soft peaks form on each. Gently fold whipped egg whites into the lemon mixture, then fold in the whipped cream.

To assemble the parfaits, arrange half the berries over the chocolate mixture in each wineglass. Top with the lemon mousse, cover each one, and refrigerate for at least 4 hours. At serving time, top with additional whipped cream, if desired, and divide the remaining berries among the six chilled wineglasses.

Chinese New Year

Yuan Zhou, Julie Qi, and
Xiuzhen Xiong provide
Chinese New Year treats.

The international community in the Centre Region is strong and viable. The university draws many students who come from abroad to study and do research, bringing their own foodways and holiday celebrations. One of the most visible groups is the Chinese Friendship Association, which plans a huge Chinese New Year celebration that draws 600 revelers in conjunction with the Chinese Culture Club and the Penn State Chinese School.

Chinese New Year is a movable holiday, usually occurring between January 21 and February 19, depending on the cycle of the moon. The new moon signifies the start of the new year, a time for rebirth that is known in solar-lunar terms as "Beginning of Spring." Before the holiday, which can be celebrated for as little as two days and as long as two weeks, families clean house to get rid of any ill fortune and to make way for all the good luck that is coming their way. Special foods that ensure good luck are eaten, and when family members come to the table, no one is allowed to bring any ill will.

Penn State graduate student Yuan Zhou and her mother visiting from Shanghai, Xiuzhen Xiong, prepared holiday dishes for a group of Chinese friends in her Eastview Terrace apartment. Yuan's daughter, Julie Qi, helped to serve and kept the guests entertained with her infectious excitement. Just before the holiday, the Asian markets in town are as busy as American grocery stores the day before Thanksgiving. People are buying all the special foods to guarantee their luck for the year. Dumpling wrappers are in high demand, because the pork dumplings are eaten for breakfast on New Year's Day.

Happy New Year, Chinese-style! Xin Nian Hao! Gou Xi Fa Ci!

Xiuzhen Xiong's Chinese Dumplings *(Jiaozi)*

MAKES ABOUT 5 DOZEN

FILLING:

3 stalks Chinese cabbage, finely chopped

2 scallions, finely chopped

1 tablespoon soy sauce

1 teaspoon salt

1 tablespoon cornstarch

¾ pound lean ground pork

¼ pound shrimp, finely chopped

⅛ pound mushrooms, finely chopped

1 10-ounce package prepared dumpling wrappers

SAUCE:

¼ cup soy sauce

2 tablespoons rice vinegar

optional seasonings: hot chili oil, grated ginger, scallions

Combine all filling ingredients in a large bowl. Place 1 teaspoon filling on each wrapper. Fold the wrappers into half circles. Moisten the inside edges with water and press them together to seal. In a large pot, bring 2 quarts of water to a boil. Drop in 12 dumplings and cover. When the water resumes boiling, add 1 cup cold water. Repeat this step twice.

When the water boils for the third time, the dumplings will be done. Combine soy sauce and vinegar to make sauce, adding seasonings like hot chili oil, ginger, and scallions if desired. Serve the sauce on the side. Repeat the cooking method until all the dumplings are cooked.

Groundhog Day

Nut roll is a Punxsutawney favorite.

Central Pennsylvania is the weather capital of the world on February 2, when all eyes turn to the small town of Punxsutawney, located about two hours west of the center of the state. Even though the number of vigilants who stomp all night on Gobbler's Knob to keep their feet warm has increased from several hundred to several thousand since the release of the popular 1993 movie with Bill Murray, the event maintains its down-home charm, thanks to the warm welcome that the residents of Punxsutawney extend.

I had always been curious about the event, but after I discovered an intriguing cookbook by Elaine Light, The New Gourmets & Groundhogs and the Second Helping, *first published by Groundhog Press in 1968, I vowed to see for myself. Driving over Route 322 in the moonlight, traversing the glistening snowbanks of the Allegheny Plateau through villages named Panic and Desire, I found my way to the Knob just before dawn. A polka tune was blasting, and people clapped their hands and stomped their feet to the beat on the frozen ground. Folks were waving and hugging and holding up signs for the television cameras. As the sun came up, one of the tuxedoed, top-hatted Inner Circle members knocked loudly on the burrow. "Give us the hog!" roared the crowd. The handler, with his elbow-length leather gloves, opened the small door and pulled out a reluctant Phil. The crowd went wild. He held him above his head. We were ecstatic! In the familiar arms of his handler, Phil relaxed and whispered his prognostication to the interpreter. He had seen his shadow—six more weeks of winter. Surprise!*

Leaving, I fell into a fast-moving lane of cars that wound down the hill to the local country club, where a breakfast buffet was waiting to warm the masses. I stood in line behind two foreign exchange students from Brazil, who said they were there because they had always heard about Punxsutawney Phil at home and wanted to see what the story was. They were happy they did. A couple from eastern Pennsylvania stood behind me. When I asked them why they had come, the man replied, "How often do you get to be a part of a folk legend?"

About the Legend

The origin of the groundhog tradition is the Christian religious festival of Candlemas Day. An old European belief is that hibernating animals, especially badgers, wake up on Candlemas Day, February 2, to take stock of winter. If the day is sunny, the animals are frightened by their shadows and crawl back into the earth for another forty days. If it is cloudy, the animals stay aboveground. German settlers to the area transferred the forecasting power to the most likely—and most abundant—candidate. The "Seer of Seers" was born.

About the Book

The next two recipes are from The New Gourmets & Groundhogs *and are used by permission of the author, Elaine Light. The cookbook itself is a treasure, and it explains the groundhog tradition in detail. The recipes combine a down-home folksiness with a sophisticated palate nurtured by plenty of worldwide travel. One of its basic premises is that "people in small towns cook better, and certainly more often than their city counter-parts." Why? "One reason is necessity. Fine restaurants are many miles away. Those who would dine well must dine at home or at the homes of their friends. The country cook is still surrounded with the essential of all good cooking, fine ingredients."*

Tips

Elaine's advice for success: Be sure to use a dark molasses for the dough. Chill the dough overnight before rolling out. Roll the dough out over plastic wrap, or on a pastry cloth.

Don't forget to brush the cookies with egg wash. The finished product has a wrinkled, furry appearance when you do this. If you forget, the cookies stay smooth and do not look as interesting. Experiment by leaving one or two unbrushed to see the difference.

Groundhog cookie cutters can be purchased from the Easter Seal Society in Punxsutawney.

Cook's Note

For a dessert in the spirit of the celebration, buy vanilla ice cream in a round quart container. Cut the container along the side, slice off a round disk of ice cream, and put it on a serving plate to suggest the frozen land- scape at Gobbler's Knob. Place a cookie on the ice cream and drizzle chocolate sauce behind it to suggest a shadow.

Elaine Light's Spicy Groundhog Cookies

MAKES 3 TO 4 DOZEN SMALL COOKIES, OR 12 TO 15 LARGE ONES

On my first magical trip to Punxsey, I walked around town after breakfast and looked at the ice sculptures outside the Indiana University of Pennsylvania Academy of Culinary Arts. The students were handing out these little cookies shaped like groundhogs, and they were excellent! Subsequent trips, however, have failed to track any of these down. There are plenty of groundhog-shape cookies, but they are of the supermarket quality—thick, pale, and overly sweet. Elaine Light developed this recipe after a dozen attempts. These cookies are distinctive and well worth the effort.

2	cups sifted all-purpose flour
½	teaspoon salt
½	teaspoon baking soda
1	teaspoon baking powder
1	teaspoon ground ginger
1	teaspoon ground cloves
1½	teaspoons cinnamon
½	cup soft butter
1	cup sugar
½	cup molasses
1	egg yolk
1	egg, slightly beaten

Sift together the flour, salt, soda, baking powder, and spices. Set aside. Cream butter and sugar together until light and fluffy. Blend in molasses and egg yolk. Stir in flour mixture and mix well. Form into a ball. Wrap in plastic wrap or wax paper. Chill for at least 1 hour.

Preheat oven to 350°F. Prepare two baking sheets by lining them with parchment paper or spraying them with cooking spray or greasing them. Roll out a small amount at a time on plastic wrap or a pastry cloth to a thickness of ⅛ inch. Cut out the cookies with a lightly floured cookie cutter, groundhog-shape if possible. Place the cookies on prepared baking sheets. Brush with the lightly beaten egg. Decorate with currants for an eye, buttons, etc. Bake for 8 to 10 minutes in preheated oven. Cool slightly before removing from the baking sheet.

Mrs. Peter Lazorcak's Bohemian Nut Roll

MAKES 4 ROLLS

Elaine Light says in her book that at the holidays Punxsutawney is divided into two camps: people who make nut rolls and people who receive them. I was delighted to find this recipe in the book, which my brother, Geoffrey, thinks is better than our grandmother's version because the proportion of filling to dough is greater.

1 package dry yeast

¼ cup warm water (110°F)

1 cup plus 1 teaspoon sugar

1 cup milk

½ cup butter

1 teaspoon salt

2 eggs

5 cups all-purpose flour

nut filling

1 egg, beaten, for glaze

Dissolve yeast in warm water with 1 teaspoon of sugar. Combine milk and butter in saucepan and heat until butter has melted. Pour into a large mixing bowl. Stir in 1 cup sugar and salt and let stand until lukewarm. Beat in the eggs and the yeast mixture, then add the flour in increments. Knead in the bowl until the flour is all absorbed and the mixture comes away from the sides of the bowl. Dough will be sticky. Cover with a damp cloth. Let rise in a warm place until doubled. While the dough is rising, make the nut filling so it has time to cool.

When the dough is ready, turn it out onto a floured board and divide into four parts. Cover with a towel and let rise 1 hour. Roll each part into a 14 x 14 inch rectangle. Spread each with one-quarter of the nut filling. Roll up each like a jelly roll, tucking in the ends as you go. Place on parchment-lined, sprayed, or lightly greased baking pans and let rise, covered, for 30 minutes.

Preheat oven to 350°F. Brush with the egg wash and bake for 35 to 40 minutes in the preheated oven, or until the loaves are well browned. Allow to cool before slicing.

NUT FILLING:

4 cups shelled walnuts, ground

½ cup butter

2 cups sugar

1 cup milk

4 egg yolks

Combine ground nuts, butter, sugar, milk, and egg yolks in a saucepan. Cook until thickened, about 5 minutes, stirring constantly to prevent mixture from scorching. Cool thoroughly.

Tips

Prepare filling in advance so it is well cooled before use.

Parchment paper makes cleanup on the pans for this recipe much easier since these nut rolls invariably leak a bit and the baked-on filling is difficult to remove from the baking sheets.

Cold Season

Homemade chicken soup can help fight symptoms of winter colds.

February is high season for colds and flu in Central Pennsylvania. A cacophony of coughs, sneezes, and wheezes is heard in every public place. Unfortunately, susceptibility to colds is universal. Almost everyone in the United States has at least one cold a year. About 50 percent of the population has at least two colds a year, and about 25 percent has three or more. Rest in bed is the best mode of defense when you have that first feeling in your nose or throat. This will help your body mobilize its resources to combat the infection. Bed rest also reduces the exposure of others to your cold, which is most infectious on the first day.

Although there is no substitute for your doctor when you have complications or prolonged symptoms, for a standard, garden-variety cold there are folk remedies that people have been using for centuries to fight infection. Best known of these is chicken soup, or "Jewish penicillin." Medical research has proven that chicken soup can indeed help to cure, or at least diminish, the uncomfortable symptoms of a cold. According to my Jewish sister-in-law, a former State College resident, the critical ingredient is chicken feet, which make a very gelatinous and yellow broth.

Another curative is "Russian penicillin," or garlic. One folk remedy is to keep a peeled clove of garlic in the mouth between the cheek and the teeth. This cure may work best on your friends—by keeping them away.

The Cure

MAKES ONE

1 tablespoon honey

1 tablespoon brandy, rum, or whiskey

8 to 10 ounces boiling water

    juice of 1 lemon

Combine all ingredients in a mug and drink while warm.

Barbra Quinn's Jewish Penicillin

MAKES ABOUT 1 GALLON

1 whole chicken, cut up

3 to 4 chicken feet (or substitute chicken wings or necks)

1 bunch parsley

1 bunch fresh dill

1 or 2 parsnips

1 or 2 turnips

2 carrots

1 onion, cut in half with outer brown skin left on

2 stalks celery

1 to 2 teaspoons salt

1 teaspoon whole peppercorns

Place chicken pieces in a large pot and cover with 1 inch of cold water. Simmer, skimming the scum that rises, for half an hour. Add the remaining ingredients and cook slowly for 2½ hours. Skim the fat from the top, strain the soup, and debone the chicken parts when cool enough to handle. Peel and chop whatever vegetables you would like to return to the broth. Add chopped chicken and vegetables to broth and reheat to serve. Add cooked noodles or rice if desired.

Cook's Notes

Onion, in the Allium family like garlic, also has germ-fighting properties. Eat as much raw onion as you can on a green salad dressed lightly with lemon juice and olive oil.

Frozen chicken feet are available locally at Far Corners Oriental Market. They are also available from kosher butchers and from farmers that raise and sell their own chickens. Chicken wings or necks are also a good substitute and will help to make a gelatinous stock because of increased collagen content.

Tip

The terms "broth" and "stock" are used interchangeably. A broth is defined as a flavorful liquid made by simmering meats and/or vegetables. A stock is defined as a clear liquid flavored by soluble substances extracted from meat, poultry, or fish, and their bones, and from vegetables and seasonings.

Baked Whole Bulbs of Garlic

MAKES 4 BULBS

4 whole bulbs of garlic

1 tablespoon butter

½ cup chicken stock

½ cup dry white wine

4 teaspoons olive oil

½ teaspoon salt

½ teaspoon freshly ground pepper

1 teaspoon dry (or 1 tablespoon fresh) herb of your choice

Cook's Note

One bulb will serve two people. The extra roasted garlic can be refrigerated and used within a few days in any number of ways. Add some roasted garlic to mashed potatoes or to a cream sauce. Puree with a vinaigrette for an interesting salad dressing. Enrich a tomato sauce for pasta. Make a pesto with fresh mint and olive oil for lamb chops. There are endless possibilities.

Preheat oven to 300°F. Trim upper tips of garlic bulb to expose inner cloves. Choose an ovenproof dish with a lid just large enough to hold the garlic snugly. Rub with the butter. Transfer the bulbs of garlic to the baking dish. Add the chicken stock and the wine. Pour 1 teaspoon olive oil over each bulb of garlic and sprinkle with salt, pepper, and the herb of your choice. Cover with the lid, or with aluminum foil, and bake for 1 hour. Baste every 20 minutes, adding more liquid if necessary. The cloves of garlic will be soft, sweet, and creamy and will slip easily out of their skins to spread on bread.

Soup Season

Jeff Brendle, affectionately known to his friends as "Bligh," is a masterful soup maker who cooks at night to unwind from his day job in computer support at Penn State. Excited by food, he often sends me e-mails describing what he's made or is dreaming of making. His repertoire of soups is long and varied, from a chilled melon-and-mint creation for a blistering summer's day, to a three-cheese-and-onion chowder that sticks to your ribs in the winter. This Szechuan Carrot Soup is good either hot or chilled, but its spicy seasoning and bright color are particularly welcome on a dreary winter day.

Bligh's Szechuan Carrot Soup

SERVES 12 TO 16

2 tablespoons extra-virgin olive oil

1 large Spanish onion, chopped

2 ribs celery, chopped

5 large cloves garlic, minced

2½-inch piece fresh gingerroot, peeled and minced

2 pounds carrots, washed but not peeled, chopped

⅓ teaspoon crushed red-pepper flakes

white pepper to taste

7 cups hot stock (vegetable or chicken)

3 tablespoons soy sauce

3 tablespoons no-sugar-added peanut butter

2 teaspoons sugar

2 teaspoons Chinese toasted sesame oil

2 cups milk

GARNISH:

1 cup sour cream

½ cup heavy cream

thinly sliced green onion

finely chopped cilantro

Heat olive oil in a 5-quart soup pot and sauté the onion, celery, garlic, and ginger until softened. Add carrots, red-pepper flakes, white pepper, and hot stock and simmer until carrots are very tender. Puree the cooked mixture. Add soy sauce, peanut butter, sugar, toasted sesame oil, and milk. Adjust the seasoning to taste with salt and pepper.

Serve warm or chilled. Combine the amounts of sour cream and heavy cream you need to garnish the soup, depending on how many servings you need. Figure about 1 tablespoon on a 12-ounce serving. Top each with chopped green onion and the cilantro.

Tip

An immersion blender makes pureeing easy. It is absolutely the best tool for the job. You will also find it useful in the kitchen for smoothing sauces and creating silk-textured soups without needing to resort to using heavy cream.

French Influence

Maurice Philippet
presents his sophisticated
creations.

Maurice Philippet was one of the French chefs who changed the style of food in Central Pennsylvania in the late 1970s and early 1980s. Anyone in State College at that time remembers with longing the days of La Chaumière and Le Bistro, which took over the Meyer's family restaurant site, where Café 210 West is presently located. I can still taste the seafood crepes, which were my favorite dish there.

I first met Maurice at a party, where he had gravitated toward a tray of raw oysters and was opening them with an expert twist, offering them to other guests with a twinkle in his eye. Dressed in denim and clogs, he seemed French from Marseilles rather than the Champs Elysées.

Actually, he is French from Algiers, where he grew up cooking from the age of thirteen. Maurice's image of the kitchen with flashing knives and gleaming copper was a vivid one. "In Europe the apprentice system teaches kitchen basics," Maurice explained with a thick French accent. "You start at the bottom—washing dishes, polishing copper—and, if you are good, you work your way up."

Work his way up he did—to become part owner of the Victorian Manor in Lemont, a name synonymous with excellent food and elegant dining.

Maurice is retired from professional kitchen duties for the present, though he still makes dinner almost every night for his Brazil-born wife, Jussara, who is assistant director of client services in executive education at Thunderbird, the American Graduate School of International Management in Glendale, Arizona. They now reside in Phoenix.

Maurice Philippet's Halibut Niçoise

SERVES 2

1 leek

1 carrot

1 tablespoon olive oil

1 tablespoon butter

2 6-ounce halibut steaks, lightly pounded

2 tablespoons flour

4 ounces mushrooms, sliced

2 ounces white wine

2 ounces capers and juices

1 clove garlic, chopped

1 tablespoon minced parsley

lemon half for garnish

Cut the green part of the leek into slivers and julienne the carrot. Blanch the vegetables in boiling water, then drain and cool. In a heavy sauté pan, heat olive oil and butter. Flour the fish on both sides and slowly sauté until the fish is opaque and slightly brown on the exterior. Remove the fish and place on a warmed serving platter.

Briefly sauté the mushrooms, and deglaze the skillet with the white wine and the caper juice. Add the capers, chopped garlic, and parsley and reduce. Garnish the fish with the blanched vegetables and pour the sauce on the fish. Serve garnished with the lemon.

Tip

Slightly pounding the halibut steaks allows them to cook evenly and more quickly.

Cook's Note

Capers are the pickled flower buds of a Mediterranean bush. They impart a lively flavor to a dish. I have a young friend, Jane Hargrave, who used to call them "salt balls" and especially loved any dishes that her mother, Nina Morgan, made with capers. Chopped green olives can be substituted, with some compromise of the finished product.

Valentine's Day

Clare Traynor pipes whipped cream on chocolate desserts.

Clare Traynor's kitchen in Pleasant Gap is a cozy one, with a basket of freshly baked carrot cupcakes at hand and a kettle on the stove ready for a quick cup of tea. Proprietor of a home-based baking business, Sweet Indulgence Desserts, the baker provides area restaurants, coffee shops, and caterers with professional-quality desserts that she makes in her own state-licensed kitchen. She also bakes wedding cakes and spends a great deal of time meeting with brides-to-be to discuss the cake that will fulfill their dreams on that special day.

A Long Island native, Clare discovered the passion that would guide her life while working as the bakery manager for the Hotel State College after a circuitous route through many commercial kitchens.

Many other bakers are licensed in Central Pennsylvania and have a home business that provides an income without punching the clock in another locale. Kim Morrison has a business, Cakes for Occasions, that provides stunning works of art for special events. With decorations that attain a level of high art, Kim has won competitions as far away as Washington, D.C., for her truly one-of-a-kind cakes.

All the bakers are busy in February, a month that includes St. Valentine's Day, a holiday devoted to proving devotion through winsome culinary treats that demonstrate affection, like Clare's Mocha Chocolate Chip Pound Cake.

Clare Traynor's
Mocha Chocolate Chip Pound Cake

SERVES 12

Clare created this recipe for a Nestlé's Toll House Morsels recipe contest and received a special recognition award.

- 1 pound unsalted butter
- 3 cups sugar
- 6 eggs
- 1 cup strong (double-strength) coffee, cooled
- 2 teaspoons pure vanilla extract
- 4 cups unbleached all-purpose flour
- 1 tablespoon baking powder
- 1 cup chocolate chips

Preheat oven to 350°F. Butter and flour (or spray) one full-size bundt or tube pan. Cream together the butter and sugar in an electric mixer. Add the eggs, one at a time. Mix cooled coffee and the vanilla. Sift together the flour and the baking powder. Add the dry and the wet ingredients to the butter-egg mixture alternately, beginning and ending with the dry. Fold in the chocolate chips. Pour into the prepared pan. Bake for 1 hour, or until tested with a toothpick that comes out dry. Cool in pan for 10 minutes, then turn out onto a cooling rack. Allow to cool completely before slicing.

Annual Chili Cook-Off

Don Plotts ladles up his
award-winning chili.

A unique event in Central Pennsylvania is the annual Chili Cook-Off at Mike and Dot's in Mifflinburg. It is a most uncommon fundraiser because rather than focusing on the well-to-do, it taps into the generous spirit of working people in the down-home surroundings of a neighborhood pub. The goal is to raise money for cystic fibrosis research. Auctioneer and co-owner Bill Cooper is a one-man show as he gently goads the crowd into ever higher bids on memorabilia items.

One repeat contestant has entered the contest four out of the ten years it has taken place—and garnered a title or placement in three of the four years. Don Plotts, who works at the post office at University Park during the day, commutes an hour each way to Mifflinburg, where he lives. He has a close connection to Mike and Dot's. His parents are Mike and Dot Plotts, proprietors of the establishment from 1972, when it was an ice-cream stand, through 1988, when they sold it to Bill and Leslie Cooper. In 1974 it became the first licensed bar and restaurant in Mifflinburg, though Don remembered that it took a few years before the concept caught on with the local population. Don cooked at the restaurant until the Coopers bought it.

At home, Don makes a cornbread to accompany his signature chili dish, often with cheese and jalapeño peppers. The recipe on the next page is the basic recipe for his winning 1998 chili entry, when he regained his chili crown.

Don Plotts's Make-Your-Own Chili

SERVES 8

Takes 1 hour to make, from start to finish.

1 pound of ground meat (any kind you like; Don likes to use hot sausage)

3 cloves garlic, chopped

1 medium sweet pepper, any color, chopped

1 medium onion, chopped

3 cans (11 to 16 ounces) of beans (mix any kind you like: kidney, black, pinto, garbanzo, great northern)

1 11-ounce can corn

2 14½-ounce cans diced tomatoes, undrained

1 8- to 10-ounce can of tomato sauce (or substitute different types of spicy vegetable juice)

1 4-ounce can tomato paste

¾ to 1 cup of liquid (water, beer, red wine— any combination)

1½ tablespoons chili powder

1 teaspoon oregano

½ teaspoon basil

additional cayenne pepper for more fire, to taste

Brown the meat with garlic, peppers, and onion. When cooked, add remaining ingredients and cook until well blended, about 30 minutes. Serve with hot cornbread.

Tip

If using dried beans in a chili recipe, be sure they are fully cooked before adding an acid ingredient like tomatoes. Otherwise, they will never soften.

Don Plotts's Jalapeño Cornbread

MAKES TWO, 9 X 9 OR 9 X 11 INCHES

Tip

The onion and jalapeño pepper in the cornbread could be sautéed slightly in oil to mellow the flavors a bit.

½ cup yellow cornmeal

1 cup all-purpose flour

2 tablespoons sugar

1 tablespoon salt

4 teaspoons baking powder

½ cup nonfat dry milk powder

3 eggs, room temperature

1½ cups warm water (105° to 110°F)

½ cup vegetable oil

1 16-ounce can cream-style corn

3 to 8 jalapeño peppers, seeded (how many you want depends on how hot they are and on how hot you want your cornbread)

2 cups grated sharp cheddar cheese

1 large onion, chopped

grated Parmesan (optional)

Preheat oven to 400°F. Spray two 9 x 9 or 9 x 11 inch baking pans with cooking spray or grease well. In a large bowl, combine the cornmeal, flour, sugar, salt, baking powder, and dry milk. In another bowl, combine the eggs, water, and oil.

Make a well in the center of the dry ingredients and add the wet to the dry. Stir to combine, then add the other ingredients and mix together with a wooden spoon or spatula. Spread the batter in the two pans and smooth the tops. Bake for about 30 minutes, or until a toothpick inserted in the cornbread comes out clean. Sprinkle with Parmesan while warm and cut in squares to serve.

Tea Time

Harmony Joseph and John LoGalbo live in Shingletown, in a brick cottage near where the blacktop road dissolves into gravel. They call their home "Teatime Cottage" and do indeed make time every day to partake in the refined institution of proper tea.

Both retired, John from the U.S. Postal Service and Harmony from working as an assistant for Lemont artist Harold Altman, they spend a lot of time traveling and especially enjoy visiting the British Isles. Annually they make a trek to New York State for a week's worth of cross-country skiing at Garnet Hill Lodge in the Adirondacks.

Both are collectors too, and there are teapots and other tea memorabilia all over the cottage. In addition, John collects antique metal tins, 1950s-era toys, and baseball cards. Harmony cannot resist vintage hats, which she wears, well, at the drop of a hat. There are even subdivisions within her hat collection—the feathered hat collection and the beaded hat collection. Antiques are everywhere in the house, and there is more to see than the eye and mind can absorb in one visit. Although much of the house seems from a bygone era, the kitchen has been remodeled to be state-of-the-art. A serious cook, Harmony spends a lot of time in the kitchen, trying recipes and testing them on John, a serious eater.

The following recipe is Harmony's favorite recipe for scones, which she makes often. The type of tea she serves with the scones depends on her mood—as does her choice of which of their forty-three teapots to use.

Harmony Joseph savors a cup of tea.

Harmony Joseph's Tea-for-Two Scones

MAKES 8

Tip

Scones are best eaten on the day they are made, so don't plan on any leftovers.

To brew a proper pot of loose tea:

Start with freshly drawn water that you heat and remove from the burner as soon as it starts to boil.

Preheat your teapot by rinsing it with the water, then add about 1 teaspoonful of loose tea for every cup of tea you wish to make.

Add hot water.

Allow to steep for 3 to 5 minutes, pour through a strainer, and enjoy.

2   tablespoons water, boiling
1   best-quality tea bag
½   cup dried currants
1   cup flour
2   tablespoons sugar
1½   teaspoons baking powder
¼   teaspoon salt
4   tablespoons cold butter
4   to 5 tablespoons half-and-half
     additional half-and-half for brushing on top
     raw sugar for on top

Steep tea bag in boiling water for 2 minutes, squeeze out all the liquid, and pour the tea over the currants in a cup. Allow currants to macerate in the tea for a few minutes. Blend the flour, sugar, baking powder, and salt. Cut the butter into the flour mixture, using a food processor or by hand. Add the half-and-half and the soaked currants to the flour mixture and mix.

Knead lightly on a floured surface and shape into a 5-inch round that is 1¼ inches high. Cut into eight wedges. Brush with half-and-half and sprinkle with raw (coarse or turbinado) sugar. Bake at 400°F for 12 to 15 minutes, or until scones are golden brown. Serve immediately with butter and jam, using your best tea service in an exquisite setting.

Spring

Spring Recipes

Spring

*O*ne day, finally, the promise of spring is in the air. The forest floor is soft again and, nourished and protected by the winter snows, the cycle of life renews. Emergence—tiny buds appear on the branches of the forsythia, the first of the flowering shrubs, and a pale fuschia light from the redbud brightens the still-dark forest. A gradual greening transforms the fields, and streams rush with snowmelt luring eager kayakers clad in wet suits.

March is an introspective month, not yet nice enough out to be spending lots of time outdoors, but time to be thinking about it. Time to be planning a garden and planting seeds, leafing through the seed catalogs that arrived in the dead of winter. Time to be using up the provisions stored away last summer, spreading jam on soda bread and sitting back with a cup of River Shannon tea.

Spring break affects the university community and frees the students who have grown so weary of crossing the tundra-like winter parking lots on their way to early morning classes. When they return, many bronzed by trips to warmer climes, there is a definite difference in attitude. And with batteries charged by such events as fundraisers for cancer research—like the Sy Barash Regatta and the Interfraternity Council Dance Marathon (THON)—they plunge into other awakening spring *activities and events. The Women's Resource Center Twilight Dinners take place in the larger community in the spring, raising money for women and children who are victims of domestic abuse.*

St. Patrick's Day is observed in State College, whether or not Irish descent is a factor. The annual Slavic and Caribbean festivals are held at the HUB, drawing thousands of visitors from the Mid-Atlantic region for ethnic music, crafts, and food. Before long, Passover and Easter bring their own special remembrances through rituals played over and over from time immemorial. Easter-egg trees blossom in yards, a curious phenomenon that delights the children.

Trout season opens in mid-April, when fisherfolk don waders to brave the chilly streams. The Pennsylvania Fish Commission, a nationwide leader in water conservation management, maintains a standard guaranteed to preserve our resources.

The flowering trees put on their annual display, and when the oak leaves are "as big as a mouse's ear" it is time to hunt for morels. These elusive mushrooms, botanically related to truffles, defy attempts at cultivation and must be approached on their own terms. Difficult to find, they are well worth the hunt. Fiddleheads are available at this time of year in the woods, their Celtic curl tight and full of promise.

Blessedly, the lawnmowers are still quiet and the lawns are permitted to green out a bit. Look closely there for the violets that hide in the tall grass, and add some to your salads. Dandelion season gives another reason not to use chemicals on your lawn. Instead, eat the weeds. Harvested before they blossom, dandelions are a spring tonic.

Mother's Day is busy for all the restaurants and hotels in the area as families treat the one who is for the most part responsible for the day-to-day family cooking. Buffets are popular and outdo each other in magnitude and presentation.

Memorial Day, at the end of May, inaugurates the cookout season. Grills are fired up throughout the region, and methods are hotly debated over the glowing coals of a neighborhood barbecue.

Charcoal or briquettes or wood? If wood, what kind? What sauce? All fine points to be argued throughout the coming months.

In Boalsburg, the Memorial Day holiday is a time to celebrate and commemorate the town's claim to fame as the birthplace of Memorial Day. In October 1864, Boalsburg residents Emma Hunter, Sophie Keller, and Elizabeth Myers met in the village and paraded to the cemetery to decorate the graves of soldiers killed in the Civil War. Today's observance includes both solemn and festive elements. There is a race, a parade, a craft show, lots of music, a pie contest, a spelling bee, and a soup and bread sale—activities to entertain all members of the family for the entire day. The most moving spectacle is the Civil War reenactment that brings reenactors from across the state to light the cannons and memorialize the sacrifices made by early Pennsylvanians so many years ago.

Spring means baseball season to many in the Centre Region, and leagues are in the fields as soon as the snow melts (sometimes before) and throughout the summer. The crack of the bat can be heard in all the recreation facilities, and a passion for the game is instilled in even the smallest uniformed player.

This is the flowering time in Central Pennsylvania, and the bulbs so carefully planted in the fall put on proud displays. On the grapevine, the growing leaves are edged with pink, and the embryonic grapes are all utterly perfect, with tiny delicate tendrils that reach out to grab hold like a baby's fingers.

From deep within the sap surges upward,
Now reaching for sugar moon.
Trees glow with a pink halo then
burst forth with a green promise soon.

The Welsh and the Irish

March 1 is St. David's Day, the national holiday of the Welsh people. Local folks of Welsh descent gather annually around this time to celebrate their cultural heritage and maintain their common bond. Margaret Knott, a Welsh woman who has been living in the Centre Region since 1977, helps to organize the annual meal that features traditional Welsh foods. "There isn't a large Welsh population in the area," says Margaret, "and our numbers are dwindling some as we all get older, but we meet so that we can remember and celebrate our common history. The tradition started here around 1960, and a group has met every year since then." The Welsh are a Celtic tribe that has always maintained its identity. The red dragon on the Welsh flag symbolizes a tenacity that endures. The Welsh national symbols are leeks and daffodils, two eternal signs of spring.

Traditional Welsh cuisine is plain but substantial fare that reflects a rural way of life. The harvest of land and sea provided the food for the predominately agricultural society, with an emphasis on fish, pork, or goat. In the small cottages where the laborers lived, food was cooked over an open fire, with a cooking pot and teakettle suspended above the flames. The griddle or bake stone was an important piece of kitchen equipment, used to make pancakes, scones, oatcakes, pastries, and the national snack, Pice Ar Y Maen, or Welsh cakes. These are eaten with tea in the afternoon to fortify body and soul. The menu for St. David's Day may change over the years, but it always includes a leek soup and tasty Welsh cakes.

Margaret Knott's Welsh Cakes

MAKES 2 DOZEN

3 cups flour

1 cup sugar

½ teaspoon salt

2 teaspoons baking powder

½ teaspoon nutmeg

1 cup butter or margarine

2 eggs

2 teaspoons milk

1 cup currants (if substituting raisins, chop finely)

Tip

An electric griddle works well for Welsh cakes because it maintains an even heat with no hot spots.

Mix flour, sugar, salt, baking powder, and nutmeg together in large bowl. Cut butter or margarine into flour mixture. Beat the eggs together with the milk and add to the dry ingredients. Add currants and mix well, using hands. Turn out onto a floured pastry cloth or cutting board. Roll out to ¼ inch thick and use a biscuit cutter or the top of a glass or jar 2½ to 3 inches in diameter to cut out circles.

Cook over medium heat on a very lightly greased or sprayed griddle or cast-iron skillet for 2 to 3 minutes on each side. Lower heat if they brown too quickly, for the inside must have time to cook. The cakes should have a brittle, sandy texture. Eat as they are or with butter, jam, or honey.

Centre County residents with Irish roots include Maureen Ferrie, who left Ireland in 1985 and traveled around the world before settling into a rambling old farmhouse in Unionville with her two cats. While working part-time at the Gamble Mill Tavern she became friends with local cook Tom Douthit, who was enchanted by tales of her homeland. He visited Ireland himself and stayed with Maureen's father, a retired shipwright. Questioned about the best food he tasted during his trip, Tom answered without hesitation, "Whatever Mo's father cooked for me!"

A local cook who has worked his way up through the ranks at many fine restaurants, Douthit was first inspired when he worked at Robert's under chef Rob Moir. He also worked at The Governor's Table, Schnitzel's, and the Gamble Mill Tavern in Bellefonte, the Allen Street Grill in State College, and the Hummingbird Room in Spring Mills. Each move has sharpened his culinary skills and deepened his understanding of the restaurant business.

Tom Douthit serves Irish Potato, Leek, and Bacon Soup to Maureen Ferrie.

Tom Douthit's Irish Potato, Leek, and Bacon Soup

SERVES 6

3 pounds potatoes

1 pint heavy cream

¼ pound bacon, diced

1 leek, white part only, sliced, washed, and diced

salt and pepper to taste

chopped fresh parsley for garnish

Tip

An easy way to rid leeks of their dirt and sand and still maintain the integrity of the vegetable is to rinse the outside of the leek, trim off the root end, then slice as much of the white part as needed. Separate the slices into rings and soak in cool water to cover for a few minutes, then drain in a colander. With this method, there is no need to slice the vegetable lengthwise and ruin the shape.

Peel 2 pounds of the potatoes and cook in sufficient water to cover until soft. Pour off half the cooking water from the potatoes and reserve. Puree the cooked potatoes and the remaining water, add cream, and simmer for 5 minutes, then set aside (this is the soup base). Peel and dice the remaining pound of potatoes. Cover with water and boil until cooked but still firm. Drain and hold.

Sauté diced bacon until brown, remove from pan with a slotted spoon, and sauté diced leeks (well washed) in bacon fat until soft. Add cooked diced potatoes, bacon, and leeks to the soup base. Season to taste with salt and pepper. If too thick, thin with reserved potato cooking water or additional cream. Serve hot, garnished with parsley.

Joann McPartland Dornich is a sprightly woman who delights her friends with authentic Irish soda bread every year in mid-March. A native of New York City, Joann has lived in the Centre Region since 1983 and currently works at Penn State with the international graduate student housing program. With her smile almost as wide as she is tall, she is the perfect representative to welcome students from other countries and assist in their orientation. A longtime member of the local herb society, she is also active in the Rotary Club. She often entertains with the help of her husband, Bob, and two sons, Kyle and Brendyn. The following recipe is from Joann's repertoire and adds an Irish-roots bacon flavor to an interesting springtime vegetable salad.

Joann Dornich totes a basket of rustic loaves.

Joann Dornich's Roasted Asparagus with Bacon-Shallot Vinaigrette

SERVES 10 TO 12

3 pounds slender asparagus

1 tablespoon olive oil

¼ teaspoon salt

DRESSING

4 slices smoked bacon

½ cup cilantro, chopped

2 large shallots, minced

¼ cup extra-virgin olive oil

4 tablespoons fresh lemon juice

1 tablespoon balsamic vinegar

1 teaspoon Dijon mustard

½ teaspoon salt

¼ teaspoon freshly ground pepper

Heat oven to 500°F. Trim asparagus ends and toss spears with 1 tablespoon olive oil. Arrange in a single layer in one or two jellyroll pans, sprinkle with ¼ teaspoon salt. Bake until tender and browned, about 10 minutes, turning asparagus once. Can be cooked several hours ahead; hold at room temperature.

For dressing, cook bacon until crisp, drain well and crumble. Add cilantro and mix well. Mix shallots, olive oil, lemon juice, vinegar, mustard, salt and pepper.

To serve, arrange asparagus on a large platter. Drizzle with dressing and sprinkle bacon-cilantro mixture on top.

Joann Dornich's Irish Soda Bread

MAKES 1 ROUND LOAF

This recipe is from Joann's mother's mother, Grandma Bridget, and makes for a flavorful, rich loaf made more enticing with the currants and caraway seeds.

3 cups sifted flour (can use half whole wheat and half white)

3 tablespoons sugar

1 tablespoon baking powder

½ teaspoon baking soda

½ teaspoon salt

1 cup currants or raisins

2 teaspoons caraway seeds

1⅓ cup buttermilk

GLAZE:

2 tablespoons sugar

2 tablespoons hot water

Preheat oven to 375°F. Sift flour, the 3 tablespoons of sugar, baking powder, baking soda, and salt into a medium-size bowl. Mix in currants and caraway seeds. Add buttermilk and mix until well blended (dough will be sticky).

Turn out onto a lightly floured board and knead about 10 times. Shape into an 8-inch round loaf. Place on a greased (or sprayed or parchment-lined) baking sheet. Cut a cross (+) into the top of the loaf with a sharp knife. Bake for 45 minutes. Dissolve sugar for the glaze in the hot water in a cup and brush generously over the hot loaf. Bake 10 minutes longer until a rich golden brown.

Sugar Moon

In the early spring there is a quiet drip-drip-drip in the forest surrounding Shaver's Creek Environmental Center. Starting in late February, the maple trees are tapped and hung with buckets to collect the sap, which falls drop by precious drop. By March, enough sap has been collected for the center to hold its annual Maple Harvest Festival. Outdoors, under the protective tarp of the "sugar shack," the collected sap is poured into a large, flat evaporator pan set over a raging wood fire. This boils for many hours, with the rising foam skimmed off continually until it is reduced. Then the "almost syrup" is taken indoors to be finished off on the stove, where the heat can be more carefully controlled. Eventually, every forty gallons of colorless, slightly sweet sap is transformed into one gallon of pure, amber maple syrup.

Native Americans were the first to harvest the bounty of the maple trees. They celebrated the "maple moon" or the "sugar moon" at the return of spring. The Indians condensed the sap by dropping heated stones in wooden troughs containing the sap.

Sugar maples abound in North America, which has the necessary climatic conditions in the spring. Frosty nights and warm days favor the flow. The harvest season lasts from around George Washington's birthday (February 22) until late March or early April—until the trees begin to bud and the sap turns yellow and bitter. The sugar in maples is synthesized by the leaves soaking up sunshine during the summer and producing starch, which is stored by the tree for the next season. This starch is the food of the plant, and in the spring, with the further action of sunlight, it is converted into sucrose and in turn to invert sugar.

Maple sap is collected drop by drop, then boiled down in flat evaporator pans outdoors in the sugar shack.

Hospitality is always in season at area bed-and-breakfasts, where the welcome mat is constantly out. Kate Kissell, innkeeper at Nittany Meadow Farm in Boalsburg, has tamed the rambling 1815 homestead on U.S. Route 322 near the Elks Club complete with barn and several outbuildings. In her country kitchen, between the commercial refrigerator and the restaurant-style coffee machine, she keeps a large glass jar of fresh chocolate chip cookies on hand for arriving guests, or for her five children who dash through the heart of this busy home.

Kate Kissell's Maple Apple Pie

SERVES 8

This apple pie is a Kissell family favorite.

Tip

With a family rental business to run, a bed-and-breakfast to take care of, and five children to keep up with, Kate is one busy woman. Her tip is to have a store-bought piecrust on hand for when company is expected or the spirit moves to make a pie. It's fine to use shortcuts that streamline the preparation—and make it that much easier to have the smell of an apple pie in your home.

¾ cup finely crushed gingersnaps

½ cup sugar

½ cup chopped walnuts or pecans

½ cup butter, melted

1 tablespoon all-purpose flour

½ teaspoon ground cinnamon

⅛ teaspoon salt

6 to 8 cooking apples, cored, peeled, and thinly sliced

1 or 2 nine-inch unbaked pie shells

⅓ cup maple syrup

Preheat oven to 350°F. Combine crushed gingersnaps, sugar, walnuts or pecans, melted butter, flour, cinnamon, and salt. Set aside. Spread half the apples in the pie shell. Spread half the gingersnap mixture over the apple layer. Repeat with remaining apples and gingersnap mixture. Top with lattice crust, if desired, or bake without a top crust. Bake for 50 minutes. Heat maple syrup to boiling and pour over the pie. Bake for 15 minutes more. Allow to cool somewhat before serving.

Coffee Czar Bill Clarke

Bill Clarke, owner of the Cheese Shoppe on Calder Way since 1976, has long been a major influence on the high quality of culinary life that we enjoy here in the Centre Region. He provides integral ingredients—cheese, coffee, and condiments—that necessitate a stop at the Cheese Shoppe for every gourmand within a fifty-mile radius. In addition to being the only European-style cheese purveyor in Central Pennsylvania, Bill's shop is a watering hole for merchants and shoppers alike in the busy Calder Alley district.

Bill Clarke sips coffee in front of the roaster.

Although he doesn't officially open until 10 A.M., self-serve coffee patrons drop by long before that, grabbing their coffee and leaving payment on the counter whether someone is there or not. A few tables in the front accommodate lingerers, but most are townspeople on their way to work. The coffee selection is always intriguing, and the dimly lit, no-frills atmosphere is somehow just right early in the day.

The coffee craze that started in Seattle in the early 1980s finally caught up to State College in 1990 when Bill started receiving 1,500-pound shipments of green coffee beans and bought a roaster. He roasts the beans as necessary to keep his supply fresh, and the aroma permeates the downtown district.

Commercial coffee, the type available in supermarkets already ground and packaged, is typically made from Coffea robusta, *a bean variety that grows well at lower altitudes. Specialty coffees are produced from* Coffea arabica, *a variety that grows at very high elevations, usually 4,000 to 6,000 feet. Roasting develops the inherent flavors and aromas of coffee beans, when the natural sugars caramelize and the green beans darken. During roasting, virtually odorless green coffee beans are exposed to temperatures between 400° and 500°F for about 5 minutes. Dark roasts are produced by holding the beans in the roaster for a longer time or by adjusting the temperature. The roasting process triggers chemical reactions that can continue for days or weeks after the roasting is completed. The chemical changes eventually lead to staleness unless the beans are handled properly. Beans should be stored in an airtight container to prevent oxidation, or they can be frozen for longer storage.*

Tip

Don't remove frozen coffee beans daily from the freezer because the freeze-thaw can cause moisture to condense on them and result in deterioration. Buy freshly roasted beans if at all possible. If you must purchase in bulk, use the freezer for storage but remove a week's supply at a time and store in an airtight container in a cool, dark place.

Kate Kissell's
Coffee Ice-Cream Punch

MAKES 24 FOUR-OUNCE SERVINGS

This festive punch for a crowd is rich enough to stand on its own as a dessert. One of Bill Clarke's special coffees makes it even better. Ice cream and milk from Meyer's Dairy make it especially delicious.

Kate Kissell spoons out some Coffee Ice-Cream Punch.

1 quart vanilla ice cream
3 cups milk
¼ cup sugar
1 teaspoon vanilla
¾ teaspoon ground nutmeg
6 cups freshly brewed coffee, cooled
Coffee Ice Cubes
whipped cream

Spoon ice cream by tablespoons into a large punchbowl. Add milk, sugar, vanilla, and nutmeg; stir until just combined. Stir in cooled coffee and Coffee Ice Cubes. Ladle into cups. Garnish with whipped cream, and additional ground nutmeg if desired.

Coffee Ice Cubes

Pour 2 cups cooled strong coffee into ice-cube tray and freeze.

Tiramisu

SERVES 10 TO 12

Two ingredients in this recipe require a trip to the Cheese Shoppe and a visit with Bill: rich mascarpone and bracing espresso beans. The word "tiramisu" means "pick-me-up" in Italian. This version is rich, but lighter than the traditional recipe that also uses a Zabaglione, an egg-yolk custard, mixed with the cheese.

 1 pound (2 cups) mascarpone
   (a rich and tangy Italian cream cheese)

 3 tablespoons sugar

 1 tablespoon orange liqueur

 2 tablespoons dark rum

 1 cup heavy cream

24 ladyfingers

1½ cups cold brewed espresso

 8 ounces top-quality semisweet chocolate,
   finely chopped

In a large bowl, combine the mascarpone, sugar, liqueur, and rum and beat until smooth. In a chilled bowl, using an electric mixer with chilled beaters, whip the cream until soft peaks form. Gently fold the whipped cream into the mascarpone mixture.

Pour the espresso into a cup. Lightly moisten 12 of the ladyfingers with the espresso and arrange them in a single layer on the bottom of an 8-inch-square glass cake pan. Spread half the mascarpone mixture over the ladyfingers and sprinkle with half the chocolate. Repeat with remaining ingredients. Cover and refrigerate for at least 1 hour or overnight.

Tip

If mascarpone is not available you can substitute 1 pound cream cheese at room temperature and whipped with ½ cup sour cream.

Focus on Health

Spring in the Centre Region marks a time of cancer awareness, and many community events are geared to educate the public about this invasive menace. The Sy Barash Regatta, the annual American Cancer Society dinner dance, the Fred Wedler Relay for Life, and the Cancer Society's daffodil sale are all fundraisers that take place at this time of year. The efforts to spotlight the issue open lines of communication and help fund programs of research, education, and patient services. At home, cancer prevention begins with making choices to provide oneself and one's family with a healthful lifestyle and healthful foods. Current research reveals that one-third of all cancer deaths may be related to diet. By choosing the proper foods, you may be able to reduce your risk of some types of cancer.

Cruciferous vegetables belong to a family of plants that bear flowers with four equal petals arranged crosswise. These extremely beneficial vegetables, which appear to protect against some cancers of the gastrointestinal tract, include broccoli, brussels sprouts, cabbage, cauliflower, Chinese cabbage, collards, cress, horseradish, kale, kohlrabi, mustard, radish, rutabaga, sea kale, turnip, and turnip greens.

Penn State is currently investigating the role of garlic as an anticancer agent. Nutrition department head Dr. John Milner served as investigator for a study of the role of garlic and what might increase or decrease its efficacy. Doctoral student Kun Song actually prepared his garlic in the foods lab where I work. The study found that microwave-heating or roasting garlic can diminish or destroy its anticancer activity unless the herb is chopped or crushed and allowed to "stand" for at least 10 minutes before cooking. In the case of whole, roasted garlic, anticancer activity was partially retained if the top of the bulb was sliced off before heating. According to Song, the 10-minute "standing time" after chopping enables an enzyme naturally present in certain garlic cells to come in contact with and act on chemicals in other cells. Chopping or crushing the garlic opens the cells and enables the enzyme to start a reaction that produces chemicals called allyl sulfur compounds, which possess anticancer properties.

Oven-Baked Chicken Dijon

SERVES 6

3 whole chicken breasts, boned and skinned

salt and freshly ground pepper

⅓ cup Dijon mustard

⅔ cup plain low-fat yogurt

3 cloves of garlic, crushed and allowed to stand for 10 minutes

1 cup bread crumbs

1 teaspoon Herbes de Provence (or 1 teaspoon total mixed thyme, rosemary, bay, lavender, and oregano)

Preheat oven to 350°F and lightly spray a baking tray with cooking spray. Cut chicken breasts in half and remove connective tissue. Flatten slightly with a mallet between two sheets of parchment or waxed paper so the cutlet will cook evenly. Sprinkle chicken lightly with salt and pepper. Mix mustard, yogurt, and garlic together and place in a shallow container large enough to hold one of the cutlets (cake pans work well). In another cake pan, mix the bread crumbs, the herbs, ½ teaspoon salt, and ¼ teaspoon pepper.

Dip each piece of chicken into the mustard-yogurt mixture, then pat both sides in the bread-crumb mixture. Place chicken in a single layer on prepared baking tray. Bake for 30 to 35 minutes, until chicken is fully cooked and juices run clear.

Braised Red Cabbage

SERVES 6

1 small red cabbage, cored and shredded

2 cloves garlic, chopped and allowed to stand 10 minutes before cooking

2 Granny Smith apples, cored, peeled, and sliced

½ cup red-wine vinegar

½ cup apple juice

½ cup water

1 tablespoon honey or red currant jelly (optional)

Combine all except the honey in a heavy, nonaluminum saucepan and cook for about 1 hour over low heat until cabbage is tender. Stir occasionally. Add honey or jelly, if desired, when cabbage is finished cooking.

Tip

The acid in the vinegar in this dish maintains the bright-red color of the cabbage. Never use the trimmings from red cabbage in your stockpot when making vegetable stock, or the anthocyanin pigments may turn it an unappetizing blue color.

Tip *(left recipe)*

Japanese bread crumbs known as panko are available in Asian grocery and specialty stores. Designed as a coating, they have a remarkable ability to remain crisp and light during cooking. They are also excellent as a breading for deep-fried foods such as oysters or shrimp.

The late naturalist Evelyn Snook of Lewistown was devastated when a diagnosis of cancer shattered her self-image at age thirty-two. This vibrant woman, who lived to be eighty-four, fought back for more than fifty years using herbs in the form of living green juices and foods as her primary therapy.

"When the doctor told me I had colon cancer, it felt like all the oxygen went out of my body. I felt deflated, withered up and rotten inside. Somehow I made it home and I just sat in my rocker on the porch for the next two days, staring into space. I felt victimized by my own body, weak and helpless. Finally an elderly neighbor stopped by and left me her copy of the Bible, saying, 'When you are ready to rebuild, you will find the stones and mortar in here.'

"So I sat for another two days, reading the scriptures and finding solace in the words that helped me to realize that I wasn't the only one who had ever suffered. But I found something else in the Bible. I found an offensive against the cancer that was eating me from within; I found the will to live and fight back by eating the foods mentioned in the Bible. The Song of Solomon 2:5 reads 'Comfort me with apples,' and I resolved to do the same."

A Biblical Menu:

Courtney Confer's Lamb and Lentil Stew

Bedouin Bread

Bitter Greens Salad with Sue Haney's Lemon-Garlic Dressing
(see Summer, page 184)

Tamarah Pie

Courtney Confer's Lamb and Lentil Stew

SERVES 8 TO 10

This lamb and lentil recipe is from Courtney Confer, who makes and serves it at the Gamble Mill Tavern in Bellefonte. Both lamb and lentils are basic foods mentioned frequently in the Bible. This combination is particularly healthful because it uses a small amount of meat to make a large number of servings.

¼ cup olive oil

2 onions, diced

2 tablespoons fresh gingerroot, grated

1 tablespoon garlic, minced, allow to stand for 10 minutes before cooking

2 tablespoons olive oil

1 pound lamb, all fat and gristle removed, cut into small cubes

salt and pepper to taste

2 teaspoons cumin powder

½ teaspoon turmeric

½ teaspoon coriander

pinch of cayenne

dash of cinnamon

2 cups lentils

1 10-ounce container of frozen spinach, thawed

1 quart chicken stock

1 28-ounce can crushed tomatoes with juice

1 pound yellow squash, chopped

In a large soup pot, heat ¼ cup olive oil and sauté onion, ginger, and garlic until translucent. While that is cooking, sauté the lamb in 2 tablespoons of olive oil in a separate skillet over a medium-high heat just until cubes are browned on the outside. Season with salt and pepper. Add the spices to the onion mixture in the soup pot and stir. Enjoy the fragrance.

Add washed lentils, spinach, stock, and tomatoes and their liquid. Add the seasoned, browned lamb cubes. Cook over low heat until the lentils are tender, about 45 minutes. Add the squash when the lentils are cooked and simmer until tender, about another 15 minutes.

Cook's Notes

This stew tastes better when made the day before serving. To prevent sticking, additional stock or water may be needed when reheating.

Lentils do not need to be presoaked like many of the larger beans.

Tip

Always examine beans for stones before cooking. Since the beans are harvested mechanically, anything the same size as or smaller than the lentil can be harvested as well. Spread the lentils on a baking sheet before washing them and sort through the single layer. Then rinse and drain in a colander.

Bedouin Bread

MAKES 8 SMALL ROUND LOAVES

Tip

Use an instant-read thermometer to be certain that the temperature of the water is 110°F, which is optimal for the yeast to develop. Too high a temperature will kill the yeast and the bread will never rise.

According to Jean and Frank McKibbin in Cookbook of Foods from Bible Days, *published in 1971 by Whitaker Books in Monroeville, Pennsylvania, bread has for centuries been the "staff of life, the word of God, the body of Christ, a sign of hospitality, food for angels, a part of the Christian's daily prayer." Literally sacred to many peoples of the world, bread embodies the spirit of the earth and "breaking" it is considered by some better than cutting it, which would cut life itself. These small, round loaves of Bedouin Bread are perfect for breaking.*

1 tablespoon yeast
1 tablespoon honey
1¼ cups tepid water
3½ cups flour
1 teaspoon salt

Dissolve yeast and honey in the tepid water. Sift in the flour and salt. Mix well and knead on a lightly floured board. Divide the dough into eight pieces and shape into rounds. Roll out, or flatten with your hands, until each one is about 5 inches across and ¼ inch thick.

Place on lightly greased (or sprayed or parchment-lined) sheets. Cover with a clean towel and let rise in a warm place for 1 or 2 hours, until they are ½ to ¾ inch thick. Bake in a very hot oven (500°F) for 7 to 8 minutes.

Bitter Greens Salad

Use an assortment of curly endive, Belgian endive, radicchio, escarole, chicory, spinach, and leaf lettuces. Garnish with olives, hearts of palm, artichoke hearts, slivers of red or roasted pepper, and other vegetables as desired. Sue Haney's Lemon-Garlic Dressing (see Summer, page 184) is an especially healthful accompaniment.

Tamarah Pie

SERVES 12

Stately date palm trees are a symbol of the Middle East, and their importance in ancient cultures is well documented. Christians carry palm branches on Palm Sunday to recall the entry of Jesus into the city of Jerusalem. Jews carry the date palm during their Sukkot ceremonies to commemorate the harvest season. A Jewish symbol of grace and elegance, the date palm was called tamar, and it was so highly regarded that it became a woman's name, Tamar or Tamarah. The Bible contains nine references to women with this name. This is another recipe from Cookbook of Foods from Bible Days.

1 cup dates, pitted and cut up

1 cup water

⅓ cup sugar

3 tablespoons cornstarch

¼ teaspoon salt

1 cup nutmeats of your choice, chopped

¼ cup orange juice

1 tablespoon orange rind, grated

pastry for a two-crust pie

sour cream or whipped cream for garnish

Preheat oven to 400°F. Boil dates in the water for 3 minutes. Mix sugar, cornstarch, and salt together. Stir into dates. Boil for 1 minute, stirring constantly. Remove from heat. Add nutmeats, orange rind, and juice.

Roll out half the dough, line a tart shell with pastry dough, and pour in the date mixture. Roll out the remaining dough and cut into thin strips. Place the strips of pastry dough on top of the date mixture in a lattice pattern. Bake for 30 minutes. Allow to cool, then cut into thin slices to serve. Serve with sour cream or whipped cream, if desired.

Tip

When adding the cornstarch mixture, be sure it is well mixed into the sugar. This separates the starch granules and prevents them from lumping together.

The Twilight Dinners

Each spring since 1988, Central Pennsylvanians have had the opportunity to get to know some new people in a most refreshing and philanthropic way. The Women's Resource Center Twilight Dinners are held by members of the community and raise money for the center to provide housing for women and children displaced by domestic violence. With at least a dozen participants opening their homes each year, there are many options from which to choose.

Sometimes hosts prepare their family favorites, as when Charles and Sherrie Garoian prepared their Armenian recipes. (See Summer, page 197.) Sometimes the tastes run to the exotic, like Indian cuisine at the home of famed Indian cooking teacher Nalini Vedam, or a Japanese menu. Another cooking teacher who has participated in the Twilight Dinners is Grace Pilato, who specializes in Italian cuisine.

One year, Duke Gastiger at the popular Spats Café had the guests help prepare their own Cajun Creole feast in the commercial kitchen on a day the restaurant was closed. Spanish tapas have been a theme, as well as a menu from the "Titanic" when the movie was the rage. Continental menus as well as menus that feature local foods are always among the choices listed. The event is an especially personal one that allows a certain serendipitous interaction between, frequently, strangers who have at least two things in common: they like food, and they like to support the efforts of the Women's Resource Center.

Duke Gastiger's Confetti Rice

SERVES 4

- 2 cups vegetable stock
- 1 cup long-grain white rice
- ½ teaspoon minced garlic
- ½ teaspoon turmeric or pinch of saffron
- ¼ teaspoon salt
- ¼ teaspoon ground black pepper
- ⅛ cup each diced red pepper, green pepper, red onion, scallion

In a one-gallon stockpot, bring vegetable stock to boil. Add garlic, rice, turmeric, salt, and black pepper. Reduce to simmer, cover, and cook 15 minutes. Add remaining ingredients, fork stir and re-cover. Continue cooking for another 5 to 10 minutes, checking for doneness.

Happy Valley Cuisine

The late Dr. Stanley J. Yoder was president of the Centre County Medical Society in 1990 when the society's auxiliary published Happy Valley Cuisine Revisited, *which contained 300 recipes and line drawings of familiar landmarks. An avid hunter who used to cook an annual game dinner for eighty or so close friends at his Blue Spring Farm, Yoder was an accomplished cook who enjoyed his spacious kitchen in a barn converted into his home in Boalsburg. In a 1990 interview, Yoder discussed his food philosophy, which is similar to that of many people in the area who make the most of what is available from the region: "I like to look at a recipe and make changes as I cook, substituting what is available seasonally and locally. I like to gather wild asparagus and wild mushrooms, looking for morels always near elm trees, and I use these natural items to make my recipes more interesting."*

Stan Yoder checks out his recipe for Moshannon Lumberjack Stew.

Dr. Stanley J. Yoder's Moshannon Lumberjack Stew

SERVES 8

2 pounds boneless uncured pork, cut into 1-inch cubes

1 teaspoon salt

1 teaspoon sugar

½ teaspoon paprika

½ teaspoon pepper

1 tablespoon cooking oil

1 cup onion, sliced

1 quart green beans, diced

1 teaspoon Worcestershire sauce

1 quart chicken stock

2 cups carrots, diced

6 small white onions, peeled

3 tablespoons cornstarch

½ cup water

Season pork with salt, sugar, paprika, and pepper. Brown pork in hot oil. Add the sliced onion and sauté 5 minutes. Add the rest of the ingredients, except the cornstarch and water. Simmer, covered for 2 hours. Blend the cornstarch with the water. Stir into the simmering stew and cook for 2 to 3 minutes.

Tip

When adding the mixture of cornstarch and water, add 2 tablespoons of the hot stew to the slurry (cornstarch–water mixture) first. Then it won't make lumps when you add it to the stew.

Local Delicacies

Central Pennsylvania specialty items crown a pillar across College Avenue from the Hotel State College.

This photograph accompanied an article that discussed what to take to Florida to provide a transplanted Pennsylvanian with a taste of home. Some of the products are no longer produced, but most of them are. A mainstay is the glass bottle of Meyer's milk, produced by Joe Meyer at his dairy between State College and Boalsburg on U.S. Route 322. In 1989 Meyer's was one of just seventy-five surviving "juggers"—retail dairy outlets in Pennsylvania that once boasted 300 operations. In 1999, the number of juggers in the state was only thirty-four—they are an endangered species.

Harner Farm, between Pine Grove Mills and State College, is still producing cider, storing their apples in refrigeration units so they can continue pressing until spring. Many other tasty local products are available at the popular roadside stand, which greets every season with an eye-catching display. Another local farm operation, Way Fruit Farm, makes apple butter in four varieties—Spice, No Spice, No Sugar, and No Sugar with Spice—to please every palate.

Tait's Raspberry Shrub is still produced and is now shipped to destinations all over the world. (See Summer, page 192.) The Taits are always developing new products and have expanded their line to include many other varieties of shrub and other gourmet items from the farm.

Unfortunately, Jack and Martha Kolln are now retired from the wine-making business, but they enjoy traveling and visiting their far-flung family. Sadly, too, Daniel Barbet's line of Le Gourmet Gourmand sausages is no longer available, and neither is Mellon Produce's Back East Salsa.

The final two products are still going strong, with growing distribution. The "Stickies" produced at Ye Old College Diner, which recently underwent a major renovation, are now sold all over Pennsylvania, shipped in attractive boxes that maintain shape and freshness for a longer period of time. Herlocher's Dipping Mustard has been produced since 1978 when it was made and served at the Train Station Restaurant with hard pretzels. The mustard became a packaged product by popular demand.

Herlocher's Deviled Eggs

SERVES 6

6 eggs
6 tablespoons Herlocher's Dipping Mustard
salt and pepper, to taste
paprika for garnish

Hard-boil eggs. Cool and peel. Split eggs lengthwise. Remove yolks and put them in a mixing bowl. Add the Herlocher's Dipping Mustard and mix well. Add salt and pepper to taste. Place the seasoned egg-yolk mixture into the egg whites and sprinkle with paprika. For a thinner filling, add more mustard.

Tip

For a professional finished look, use a pastry bag with a tip to fill the egg whites. It will also be much faster.

Cook's Note

To avoid overcooking the eggs, which causes the gray-green ring to form around the yolk, bring enough water to cover the eggs to a boil. Meanwhile, warm the eggs by placing them in a bowl of warm water to cover. This will prevent them from cracking when they go into the hot water.

When the water boils, add the eggs and time them for 12 minutes once the water returns to a boil. (Always cook an extra egg or two for testing purposes.) After 12 minutes, remove one egg, chill it under cold running water for 20 seconds, then remove the shell and slice in half. If the eggs yolks are still runny, the eggs need more cooking time. Most eggs will take between 12 and 15 minutes. The fresher an egg, the less time it will take to cook. When properly cooked, pour off the hot water and plunge the eggs into a cold-water bath to stop the cooking. This will prevent the ring from forming and result in creamy yellow yolks.

Norma and Joe Bayer lead
a sweet life.

Norma and Joe Bayer lead a very sweet life that centers on their business: Bayer's Mountain Honey & Beeswax Crafts, near the intersection of Route 220 and Interstate 99 at Bald Eagle. Nestled in the woods, their stone cottage, "Edgewood," looks like something from a fairy tale, with a goat pen nearby and a fenced area stacked with white beehive boxes. Both retired from Penn State, they have been keeping bees since 1990, when Joe was charmed one day while observing a honey bee.

A brown shed near the cottage houses their small retail operation and displays a yellow sign in the window that reads "Local Honey for Sale." Inside, the walls are lined with beeswax candles, salves and lip gloss, herbal suncatchers, soaps, honey collectibles, and dozens of (mostly blue) prize ribbons won at various competitions. The rear of the shed is fitted with equipment for their avocation. A Department of Agriculture license and a Pennsylvania Pride poster, plus several posters about the life cycle of bees, are on the wall.

The Bayers aren't always in the shed, however. They frequently do educational programs at schools and for Scout and senior-citizen groups. They clearly have a sense of mission. Norma explained their urgency: "Wild bees are dying out, victims of a mite infestation. The role of the beekeeper is critical to the farmers who need the bees to pollinate their crops. Beekeepers set their hives in fields and orchards on a rotating basis as the crops flower. Even home gardeners are starting to notice lower yields because the wild bees just aren't there anymore."

Honey is a natural product that is one of nature's great gifts. In the summer there are 60,000 to 80,000 bees in a hive, all working to supply one queen, who lays 1,500 eggs a day. The worker bees live for between three and six weeks and produce just one-twelfth of a teaspoon of honey in their life spans. The queen lives about four years. It takes the nectar from two million flowers to produce one pound of honey.

Norma Bayer's Honey Applesauce Oatmeal Cookies

MAKES 3 DOZEN

¾ cup shortening

½ cup brown sugar, firmly packed

½ cup honey

1 egg

1 cup thick applesauce

1½ cups oats, quick or old-fashioned

2 cups sifted all-purpose flour

½ teaspoon baking soda

½ teaspoon cinnamon

½ teaspoon salt

½ cup raisins

Preheat oven to 375°F. Prepare baking sheets by greasing, spraying, or lining with parchment paper. With electric mixer, cream shortening until light. Add brown sugar and honey and continue to beat. Add egg and applesauce, then mix in the dry ingredients until well combined. Stir in the raisins. Drop by tablespoons onto prepared cookie sheet and bake for 12 to 15 minutes.

Tips

Generally, the lighter in color the honey, the milder the flavor.

Honey retains its flavor best when stored at room temperature.

Honey draws moisture and flavors from the air, so keep it covered when not in use.

If honey granulates, it can be liquefied again by placing the jar in warm water (not more than 130°F) for a few minutes. Honey used in baked goods will keep them fresher longer.

Honey can be measured more easily by using the fractional measure you use for the fat in a recipe, or by spraying the measuring cup with a light layer of cooking spray.

Honey can replace sugar in most recipes. Reduce the liquid by ¼ cup for each cup of honey used.

A Jewish Seder

Harriet Feinstein explains seder traditions to Mark Borowski.

Jewish mothers in the Centre Region are busy in the spring. They must clean out their kitchen cupboards and make the kitchen kosher for Passover by discarding any bread or flour and any leavening (the "hametz"). Cabinets that won't be used for the holiday are sealed, and separate linens and food preparation items are used. The restrictions help to make the holiday that much more sacred. Harriet Feinstein lives in State College and helped to supervise an annual Seder, the Passover feast, at the Jewish Community Center in 1998. It was catered by Mark Borowski, who was then a student in hotel, restaurant, and institution management at Penn State.

Passover celebrates the liberation of the Jews from slavery in Egypt. For eight days, Jews eat matzoh, an unleavened flatbread, to recall the fact that they left Egypt before the bread could even rise. All the elements of the sacred meal are spelled out in the Haggadah, a written description detailing the order and symbolism that includes the prayers said at the seder.

Mark, born in Philadelphia and raised as a Roman Catholic in southern New Jersey, looked forward to catering the dinner as a cultural experience. Hungry for knowledge, he researched and prepared the traditional meal to "broaden my knowledge of ethnic foods and give me a different perspective. I've worked with many excellent Jewish chefs, and now I can understand more where they are coming from with some of their dishes. It's all a learning experience for me."

Mark Borowski's Roasted Whole Chickens

SERVES 6

3 whole chickens, cleaned and cut in half

¼ cup olive oil (extra-virgin works best)

1 tablespoon kosher salt (see Tip on page 175)

2 teaspoons sugar

½ teaspoon ginger, ground

½ teaspoon cayenne pepper

½ teaspoon allspice, ground

6 limes

Preheat oven to 400°F. Massage chickens with half the olive oil. Mix the salt, sugar, ground ginger, cayenne pepper, and allspice and season the birds lightly with about half the mixture. Place chickens on large roasting pan in a single layer and put into the preheated oven. Squeeze the limes and set the juice aside.

After 20 minutes, remove the chickens, drizzle half the lime juice and the remaining olive oil over them, and sprinkle with the rest of the spice mixture. Return to oven. After 5 minutes, lower the temperature to 325°F and bake until done (approximately 45 minutes, depending on the size of the chicken). When the chickens register 180°F on an instant-read thermometer and the juices run clear when thickest portion is pierced with a fork, remove from the oven, pour the remaining lime juice on the crispy birds, and serve while hot.

Cook's Note

Empire Kosher is the world's largest kosher poultry-processing plant. Now located in Mifflintown, Pennsylvania, the facility has its own hatchery, feed mill, and network of local contract farmers who grow free-range chickens and turkeys that are processed according to Jewish dietary law. Empire products can be found throughout the United States and all over the world.

Another local source for chicken is Myers Brothers Meats in Spring Mills, which has excellent local poultry products. Once you are accustomed to these fine birds, you will really notice a difference in texture and flavor compared with supermarket chicken. Myers Meats supplies most of the area restaurants and O. W. Houts in State College, where the butcher-counter concept is still alive and well.

A Hindu Holi Festival

Rishi Agrawal, Natalya Lakhtakia, and Trisha Agrawal prepare for Indian Holi festivities.

The Centre Region Indian community marks the spring with the Hindu Holi festival, which celebrates the sprouting of tender leaves and the return of blooming flowers. In 1993 fifteen families gathered for an Indian potluck dinner to celebrate, but by 1998 the number in attendance had increased to 250 and the dinner was being catered by one of the new Indian restaurants in town—an indication of the rapidly increasing cultural diversity of the area. Today there is no longer a dinner. Instead, an expanded cultural program is presented to a large audience.

Organizer Sadhna Agrawal explained that Indian families also enjoy congregating to see a cultural program put on by the children in the community. At the Holi festival held at the Mount Nittany Middle School, the spacious interior is decorated and transformed into an ephemeral Taj Mahal for the day. Dressed in their finest saris, the Indian women of the community seem to sail as they walk, brilliant clouds of patterned fabric flowing behind them. They wear their finest jewelry to the festival, and the children are also dressed in traditional Indian attire. It is a time to connect with one another through ritual, to celebrate the roots of their culture, and to transplant a branch of their own tree to Central Pennsylvania.

Balwant Singh's Indian Spiced Vegetables *(Nav Ratan Korma)*

SERVES 4 TO 5

Balwant Singh is the chef at Preet Restaurant in State College, currently one of three Indian restaurants in town.

3 tablespoons oil, divided

1 large onion, diced

1 half-inch piece of ginger, minced

2 cloves garlic, minced

1 teaspoon whole cumin seeds

1 medium tomato, peeled, seeded, and diced

1 teaspoon whole coriander seeds

¼ teaspoon turmeric

¼ teaspoon red chili powder (optional)

½ teaspoon garam masala

1 cup broccoli florets

1 cup green pepper, cut into long strips

1 cup carrots, cut into ¼-inch pieces

1 cup potato, cut into ¼-inch slices

1 cup cauliflower florets

¼ cup paneer (homemade Indian cheese), cubed (optional)

¼ cup raisins

¼ cup cashews

¼ cup fresh cilantro, chopped

In large sauté pan, heat 2 tablespoons of the oil and sauté onion, ginger, and garlic with the cumin seeds until golden brown. Add the chopped tomato and the coriander, turmeric, chili powder, and garam masala.

In a separate, nonstick skillet, heat the remaining 1 tablespoon oil and add the broccoli, peppers, carrots, potatoes, and cauliflower. Stir and cook over high heat for a minute, then cover, reduce heat to medium-high, and cook for 5 minutes, or until the vegetables are tender but crisp.

Add the cooked vegetables and the paneer to the onion mixture. Add the raisins and the cashews. Salt to taste. Mix well and cover for another 5 minutes to blend the flavors. Serve hot with *naan* (Indian flatbread). Garnish at serving time with fresh cilantro.

Tip

Store fresh gingerroot in the freezer. It's easy to shave what you need from the frozen root, so there is no need to mince it.

Easter Traditions

Many people of the Christian tradition mark spring with an Easter celebration that uses eggs as the symbol of a silent universe suddenly bursting into action and light. Almost every nation has folklore associated with the egg, from creation stories to nursery rhymes. An ancient Persian story of creation centers on the hatching of the world from an enormous egg. The Persians were the first to color eggs and present them as gifts at the time of the spring equinox. There are also Hindu, Hawaiian, and Finnish creation myths involving eggs.

Since the time of Christ, the egg has assumed an even greater importance. It was used as a symbol of the new life Christians found in their Savior. Many Christians, especially those of the Eastern Orthodox faith, began the practice of giving gifts of eggs on the morning celebrating the Resurrection of Christ. The gift expressed a renewal of life through the Resurrection and a renewal of faith and love. In many countries, the eggs are dyed red in remembrance of the blood Jesus shed on the cross. The egg is also symbolic of the stone rolled away from the tomb, which is represented by egg-rolling contests and similar Easter observances.

Centre County sprouts a number of Easter egg trees in the spring, a tradition that has roots in Europe. In Germany the egg tree evolved from a secular custom of impaling uncolored eggshells of various kinds on bushes outdoors to herald the spring. By the 1890s, very elaborate Easter egg trees were popular in Germany. These were made from an evergreen like the Christmas tree and decorated with blown, dyed eggs, ribbons, candies, and cake animals shaped like rabbits and lambs. Gifts were piled underneath. Today, the German egg tree is most likely a cluster of birch or forsythia branches in a large vase decorated with blown, dyed eggs and small ornaments.

Easter dinner in many Central Pennsylvania homes includes ham, which generates many more meals than just one Easter feast, like this ham and cheese chowder from Connie Snyder.

Connie Snyder's
English Cheddar Chowder

SERVES 10 TO 12

Connie Snyder lives in Williamsport and is an extraordinary cook. Very active in the Mount Nittany chapter of the American Wine Society, she comes to State College for its bimonthly meetings. AWS meetings used to include a members' potluck, and this sharing of various appetizers was as eagerly anticipated as the meeting itself. Connie's recipes were always big hits.

2 cups water
⅓ cup carrot, finely chopped
⅓ cup celery, finely chopped
⅓ cup scallions, finely chopped
1 medium onion, finely chopped
½ cup butter
½ cup flour
4 cups milk, hot
4 cups chicken broth, hot
1 pound sharp cheddar cheese, grated
1 tablespoon Dijon mustard
salt, pepper, and cayenne to taste
¾ to 1 pound smoked ham, finely chopped
green scallion tops for garnish, chopped

In a small saucepan, bring the water to a boil and add carrot, celery, and scallions. Boil the vegetables for 5 minutes. Reserve. In a soup pot, cook the onion in the butter for 1 minute, or until wilted. Blend in flour and slowly add the hot milk and hot chicken broth. Whisk the mixture constantly until it is well blended and smooth. Add the cheese, the reserved vegetables and their cooking liquid, mustard, seasonings, and ham. Continue cooking the soup, whisking constantly, until the cheese is melted and everything is well blended. Garnish with green scallion tops.

Cook's Note

Hosterman's Market in Centre Hall is the source for smoked hams unlike any others available in the area. The hams, smoked on site, have a strong, smoky aroma that is too strong for some people. Other butchers in the area, including O. W. Houts in State College and Myers in Spring Mills, have good country hams as well.

Spinach Salad with Creamy Sweet-and-Sour Dressing

SERVES 4 TO 6

This is a great way to use some of those hard-boiled eggs. Just be certain the eggs have not been out of the refrigerator longer than two hours or left lying in the sun.

1 pound spinach

3 hard-boiled eggs

3 slices bacon, cooked crisp and crumbled

1 small red onion, cut into rings

¼ pound mushrooms, cleaned, trimmed, and sliced

4 ounces Creamy Sweet-and-Sour Dressing

Clean and remove the stems from the spinach. Place spinach in a large bowl and toss with 4 ounces of Creamy Sweet-and-Sour Dressing. Arrange the eggs, bacon, onion, and mushrooms on the top.

CREAMY SWEET-AND-SOUR DRESSING:

1 cup apple-cider vinegar, divided

2 teaspoons salt

½ teaspoon white pepper

½ teaspoon oregano

2 cloves garlic

1 tablespoon dry mustard

¼ cup honey

2 cups safflower oil

Combine ½ cup of the apple-cider vinegar, salt, white pepper, oregano, garlic, dry mustard, and honey in blender and blend until smooth. Slowly drizzle in 2 cups safflower oil while the blender is running. Add the remaining ½ cup of vinegar to the mixture in the blender and blend until fully emulsified and mixture is smooth. Makes 1 quart.

Cook's Note

White pepper is preferred over black pepper in recipes that are light in color, like cream sauces or this ivory-color dressing. Black pepper specks detract from the finished appearance. Penzey's Spices is a mail-order company that ships premium spices and herbs in both small and large quantities. The catalog itself is a wealth of information about the origins of various seasonings and contains excellent recipes.

Tip

You can also use the egg slicer, if it is sharp enough, to slice the mushrooms.

Local Cooking Clubs

Wine measurably drunk, and in season, bringeth
gladness to the heart and cheerfulness to the mind.

—ECCLESIASTICUS 31:28

*The Mount Nittany Chapter of the American Wine
Society holds an annual gourmet dinner in the spring
at Mountain Acres Lodge, a rustic hideaway in the
Seven Mountains area between Potters Mills and
Milroy. The dinner held in 1986 was a "glad" and
"cheerful" event indeed. Half the society's membership
consisted of home winemakers who showcased their
wines during the six-course gourmet meal prepared
cooperatively by the members. The meal explored the
dynamism between food and wine in its most natural
setting—on the table.*

*Regional and seasonal pairings of food and wine
have existed for centuries and are the norm in most
parts of the western world. Food and wine complement
or contrast with each other through the interaction of
acids, fats, and flavors. The goal is always balance
between the food and wine. The American Wine
Society dinner was a celebration of fine wines produced
in members' cellars to accompany gourmet foods
produced in members' kitchens. The delicate equipoise
that the food and wine pairings achieve is an annual
event eagerly anticipated by the society members.*

Jane Norris's Sesame Seed Puffs

MAKES ABOUT 24

- 1 package frozen puff-pastry sheets
- 2 bunches scallions
- 1 teaspoon salt
- 1 egg
- ⅓ cup white sesame seeds

Preheat oven to 425°F. Dust a pastry
cloth, cutting board, or countertop with
flour. Roll out puff-pastry sheets to make
an 8 x 10 inch rectangle. Chop scallions
into ⅛-inch slices, using a small portion
of the green stem. Place chopped
scallions into a small nonstick pan and
cook over medium heat for 1 minute,
stirring constantly. Add salt and cool.

With a 2½-inch cutter, cut circles
from the puff pastry. Place a teaspoonful
of sautéed scallions in the center of each
circle, fold in half, and press the edges
together. Brush semicircles with beaten
egg. Sprinkle with sesame seeds. Bake on
parchment-lined baking trays for 10 to
15 minutes until golden brown.

Tip

*Other fillings could be
used for variety: chopped
roasted red pepper, rings
of black olive, goat cheese,
crumbled sausage, or ham.
The possibilities are
endless.*

Connie Snyder's
Carre d'Agneu Dijonnaise

SERVES 8

This wonderful rack of lamb recipe also originated in the recipe files of Connie and the late Chuck Snyder of Williamsport. They orchestrated the dish at the Wine Society dinner and oversaw the cooking of the racks of lamb to absolute perfection. Connie and Chuck always brought interesting recipes and culinary tales to the club functions. Chuck was an avid hunter and specialized in preparing game dishes. They lived an epicurean lifestyle in Williamsport.

Cook's Note

Clarified butter is pure butterfat with milk solids and water removed. It is preferred for cooking because it can reach a higher temperature without sizzling and burning. It has the high-heat advantage of an oil but all the flavor of butter. Clarified butter is easily made by melting butter at a low temperature on top of the stove or in a microwave and pouring off the butterfat that collects at the top.

3   8-bone racks of lamb

flour for dredging

salt and pepper

½   cup clarified butter

6   tablespoons Dijon mustard

2   teaspoons garlic, minced

1   teaspoon shallot, minced

2   cups coarse bread crumbs

2   tablespoons parsley, chopped (or 2 teaspoons dried)

2   tablespoons fresh basil, chopped (or 2 teaspoons dried)

1   tablespoon fresh oregano, chopped (or 1 teaspoon dried)

1   tablespoon Parmesan cheese, grated

Preheat oven to 425°F. Trim racks of lamb of all visible fat and sinewy tissue. "French" the racks by removing the small bit of meat between the bones. Season the flour with salt and pepper and place on a baking tray with a rim. Dredge the racks with the seasoned flour.

Heat ¼ cup of the clarified butter in a large sauté pan over high heat. Brown the racks quickly on all sides. Remove from pan. Combine mustard with garlic and shallots. Combine bread crumbs with herbs and cheese.

Spread lamb liberally with the flavored mustard, then roll in the seasoned bread crumbs, patting firmly so crumbs adhere. Place racks on broiler pan. Moisten the crumb-coated racks with the remaining butter and roast for 15 to 18 minutes, until the meat reaches the temperature of 140°F on an instant-read thermometer for medium rare, if serving the chops immediately. Slice into the rack to check the doneness. If more doneness is desired, slice the chops, lay them on the broiler rack individually, and finish in the hot oven for a minute or two.

Il Circolo Italiano was a Penn State club that met monthly to share la dolce vita through potluck dinners and conversation, Italian-style. Fifty members and associates paid annual dues of five dollars to belong to the group. Most were actively involved in the Italian Department at Penn State, but some were just aficionados who came to speak the language and enjoy the camaraderie.

In 1997, David Cusumano of Long Island, New York, was president of the club. His parents, who operate an Italian restaurant in New York, are from Italy, and he himself is a native Italian speaker. He supervised other students preparing a chicken dish that he makes at the restaurant. Marisa DeSantis, a graduate student in Spanish and an instructor in Italian at the time, brought an intriguing roasted tomato recipe that she got from her mother, Suzanne DeSantis.

David Cusumano's Italian-Style Chicken Cutlets

SERVES 6

3 whole chicken breasts, boned and skinned

1 cup flour

3 eggs, beaten

2 cups seasoned Italian bread crumbs

extra-virgin olive oil

1 lemon

¼ cup fresh parsley, chopped

Rinse chicken breasts in cool water and pat dry with paper towels. Trim away connective cartilage and any fat. Pound the chicken cutlets with a meat mallet to an even ½ inch thick. Put flour onto a rimmed plate and press each pounded chicken cutlet thoroughly into it to coat with a dusting of the flour.

Place beaten eggs in shallow dish and put seasoned crumbs in adjacent shallow dish. Dip flour-coated cutlets into beaten egg, then immediately into the bread crumbs to coat each side of the cutlet. Place cutlets on waxed-paper-lined baking sheets while you get them all ready; chill for a few minutes.

Pour the olive oil in a sauté pan to ¼-inch thickness and heat over medium-high heat. When the oil is hot, sauté each cutlet for about 3 minutes on each side. Hold finished cutlets in a warm (200°F) oven until all the frying is completed. Garnish with a lemon wedge and a sprinkling of fresh parsley.

Tip

Pound the cutlets between two sheets of parchment paper or waxed paper to reduce tearing the flesh. Also, this is much neater and makes cleanup easier. Use cake pans for holding the egg and crumbs to dip the chicken. It is easier to dip them into a wide, shallow container.

Marisa DeSantis's Twice-Roasted Plum Tomatoes

MAKES ABOUT 2 QUARTS

Since encountering this dish, I am rarely without a jar of it in my refrigerator when garden tomatoes are out of season. It is a perfect food—easy to prepare, good at any mealtime, low in fat, and good for you.

3 pounds plum tomatoes

   extra-virgin olive oil

   minced garlic (already prepared, in a jar)

2 teaspoons salt

2 teaspoons pepper

1 tablespoon dried rosemary

Preheat oven to 375°F. Slice plum tomatoes in half lengthwise and place on two large baking trays. Place ¼ teaspoon minced garlic and ½ teaspoon olive oil on each tomato half and sprinkle both trays with the salt, pepper, and rosemary. Cook, uncovered, for about 30 minutes, or until tender (older tomatoes take longer). Remove from baking sheet and place into a large roasting pan. Pour on an additional ½ cup of olive oil and bake uncovered for another 30 to 45 minutes, or until the tomatoes are very soft. When cool, store in a jar, covered with the olive oil in which they baked.

Tip

Streamline the method by just baking for 1 hour at 375°F and leaving them in the same pan. Also, the additional oil can be eliminated. Fresh rosemary adds a lot of flavor to the dish; use 3 tablespoons fresh to substitute for the 1 tablespoon dried.

Trout Season

Every spring people come to the Centre Region from far and wide to try their luck with some of our native and stocked species of trout. Anglers who come home with empty nets can still enjoy fresh local trout by stopping at Giant supermarket on North Atherton Street and buying some of the live trout that swim along in an adjacent tank next to the live lobsters there. Dan Brigham stocks the trout tank with his harvest of brook, brown, rainbow, and steelhead trout from Elk Creek Fisheries in Millheim, where he raises them. He also sells fresh and smoked trout during the summer months at the State College farmers' market on Fridays.

Dan Brigham stacks his smoked trout at the farmers' market.

Fish Commission Chronology :

1866

The Pennsylvania Fish and Boat Commission is born, after public outcry over pollution in the state's waters, particularly those affecting the annual shad run.

1870

Private citizen Thad Norris purchases 450 bass, taking them from the Potomac River and releasing them into the Delaware River below the Lehigh River Dam at Easton.

1875

The "Western Hatchery" is constructed in Corry on nine acres purchased for $2,000. By 1886 the first brown trout eggs—some 10,000 of them, which were purchased from Germany—hatched.

1903

The Bellefonte Hatchery opens, funded in part by the citizens of Bellefonte, who paid for the hatchery land.

1906

The Spruce Creek Hatchery in Huntingdon County is started and the foundation of aquaculture in the Centre Region is well established.

1909

Legislation makes it illegal to empty any waste toxic to fish into any waters of the Commonwealth.

1915

Fish wardens and their deputies are given the power to make arrests.

1922

Resident fishing licenses are established at $1 for adults, and the Commission becomes self-supporting when it earns $207,425.53 for the first year's sales.

1934

Centre County resident George Harvey is hired by the Commission to teach fly-fishing.

1938

The hatcheries produce their own brown and rainbow trout eggs for the first time.

1970

The brown trout is named the official state fish.

1976

The Commission begins trout stream inventory.

1985

The Commission's Cooperative Nursery Program lists 188 fish culture facilities.

1991

The Pennsylvania Fish Commission becomes the Pennsylvania Fish and Boat Commission.

2000

The daily creel limit for trout is reduced from 8 to 5; the limit was last changed in 1952.

Baked Trout

SERVES 2

Cook's Note

When choosing whole fish, look for clear, shining eyes and red or pink gills. The texture of the flesh should be firm and elastic, and there should be no "fishy" odor, which is actually a sign of decomposition. Fresh fish should smell and taste sweet and fresh.

Tip

A hemostat from a medical supply store is a good tool for gripping and removing tiny bones from both cooked and raw fish.

This is a method that can be used for any type of round fish—that is, fish that can be positioned in an upright "swimming position" after they have been gutted. The technique works for 12-pound salmon as well as for trout that weigh less than a pound. It is easy and has the advantage of being able to be done ahead so the fish can be skinned, removed from the bone, and then flashed under a hot broiler with an appropriate sauce at serving time. Fish cooked intact with bones and skin has far more flavor than fillets.

    2   whole trout
    ¼   cup dry white wine
        dill or tarragon sprigs

Preheat oven to 425°F. Line a baking tray with aluminum foil, leaving long ends on either side. Rinse the fish inside and out and pat dry with paper towels. Measure the thickness of the fish at the widest point. Place the two fish on the baking tray upright in the swimming position with the belly spread out. The head of one fish should be even with the tail of the other fish for even heat distribution. Tuck fresh sprigs of dill or tarragon under the belly of each fish. Pour the wine over the two fish and put another sheet of foil on the top, crimping it very tightly so that no steam escapes.

Bake for about 10 minutes per inch. At the end of the cooking time, press through the foil to determine whether the fish is cooked enough. The flesh should feel firm. Remove from the oven and allow to stand for 5 minutes. Carefully unwrap the foil and remove fins and skin. Allow to cool for a minute, then remove the cooked fillets from the bone and place on a heated serving tray, or on a heatproof platter if you will reheat the dish at serving time with a sauce. Serve with warm melted butter and lemon wedges, or any sauce.

Anchovy Sauce for Trout

SERVES 4

I first encountered this sauce at a trattoria in Orta, an island village situated in the middle of Lake Orta near Lake Maggiore in Northern Italy. Traveling with our two small sons, we rented a rowboat to get there, and my husband, John, rowed us out to the island, working up an appetite by the time we arrived. The trattoria where we dined shared the recipe.

¼ cup olive oil, best quality

1 tin anchovies, finely chopped
(or 2 tablespoons anchovy paste)

1 garlic clove, finely chopped

1 tablespoon lemon juice

1 tablespoon capers

8 trout fillets, cooked and warm

In a small saucepan, combine oil, anchovies, garlic, and lemon juice and heat for a few minutes until the sauce is smooth. Add capers and remove from the heat. Drizzle while still warm on warm trout fillets.

Whole baked trout
garnished with flowers.

Eric Sarnow's Trout in a Potato Crust

SERVES 4

Eric Sarnow prepares food in his restaurant kitchen.

Chef Eric Sarnow and his wife, Claudia, came to the Centre Region from Philadelphia in 1993 when their son Evan was born. While Eric was challenged working as a sous chef at Le Bec Fin under celebrated chef Georges Perrier, he decided to trade that for more time with his family. Today Eric cooks in the same classical French style, and Claudia works with him supervising the front of the house in their own establishment, the Hummingbird Room in Spring Mills. They operated the first rendition of the elegant restaurant in rented space at the Woodward Inn before buying a 152-year-old farmhouse next to the Pentecostal church outside Spring Mills. After months of renovations, they opened in 1995 and have been busy ever since. Open only from Wednesday to Sunday, they maintain a normal life outside their business and have time for the usual amount of parental chauffeuring to lessons and practices for Evan.

Tip

Use a mandolin to slice the potatoes as thin as possible, so they can wrap around the fillet.

1 large russet potato, washed and peeled
4 trout fillets
  salt and pepper
  clarified butter

Slice the potatoes as thin as possible. Arrange potato slices in four areas of a flat work surface, and overlap the slices to cover an area twice as wide as the fillets, about 4 x 8 inches. Place one trout fillet in the center of each potato area. Season the fish with salt and pepper.

Roll up the trout in the potato slices to form a neat parcel. Brush the exterior with clarified butter to help the potatoes adhere to the fillets. Heat additional clarified butter in a sauté pan until the butter is hot and a few drops of water shaken onto the surface "dance." Place the trout-potato parcels in the hot butter and cook over medium-high heat until the golden brown. Do not cook at too high a heat or the trout within will not be fully cooked.

Spring Mushrooms

April 28, 1995—100 morels, not much rain
April 27, 1996—found first morels
April 26, 1997—4 morels
April 12, 1998—found 15

Dave Benner's journal tracks the cycles of the year's natural phenomena. A beekeeper, Benner notes the first blossom of the sweet cherry, the bloom of the locust, the flowering of the dandelion and clover. Tuned in to the rhythms of the season in a primordial way, he chronicles the year in terms of emergence and harvest. In the margins of his journal he keeps track of the mushrooms. "Spring gobbler season is when I usually find morels," said Dave, a native of Zion, "and that is always late April or early May." His find in 1998 was the earliest he ever recorded and caused a small uproar in the morel-hunting community. Word spread quickly—but indirectly. "They're out." "No way. Too early." "I'm holding two." "Okay." The word "morel" is better left unspoken. Information about morels is shared only with immediate intimates.

The mushrooms are so elusive and so highly prized that their apprehension signifies a victory over the forces of nature and implies a certain virility. Morel lust is easier to understand once you have tasted them. Related to their

Morels are the most highly prized spring mushroom.

French cousin, the truffle, morels have a nutty, woodsy quality. Both morels and truffles are ascomycetes—they produce spores for reproduction in a closed structure called an ascus. The morel spores develop in the pits of the honeycombed head. Morels seem impossible to tame and cultivate. Capricious, they grow where they will, though rumor has it that they prefer apple orchards, rotting wood, burned sites, and spruce or poplar woods.

Different types of morels are found in Central Pennsylvania. The black morel, Morchella elata, *is often the first true morel to emerge in the spring. The next type to appear is the yellow morel, or* Morchella esculenta. *Morels are excellent for beginning foragers because they are so recognizable. Although each may differ in size, shape, and color, they cannot be confused with any other plant. The distinguishing feature is the cone-shaped cap with irregular ridges and pits that lead to common names like "sponge mushroom" or "corncob."*

Morels stand between 1 and 6 inches high, with the cap forming the upper half to two-thirds of the mushroom and the stem the remainder. The cap ranges from yellow to tan to dark brown, with the stem somewhat paler. The important characteristic is that both the stem and the cap are hollow and have a crisp texture. False morels, Gyromitra esculenta, *have a similar though very uneven and misshapen outward appearance, but they are not hollow. A toxin known as monomethylhydrazine (MMH) is present in varying amounts in false morels and causes vomiting, abdominal cramps, and diarrhea. Some fatalities have been reported from eating false morels. It is very important to find a veteran morel-picker to guide you through your first forays—or someone you can take them to for examination.*

Many area restaurants feature morels during their month-long season, catering to those who want to taste them but either don't know where to look for them or don't have the time. Central Pennsylvania forests are sometimes thick with morel hunters, who have been known to wear camouflage to hide their presence.

John Corr's Sautéed Morels

SERVES 2

My husband and I are of opposing camps when it comes to morel cooking. He prefers them unadorned and unaccompanied. I prefer to stretch them some by sautéing them, then adding cream and reducing it to make a sauce for pasta. Because he gathers the vast majority of them, it is usually his call. I find it difficult to discern their shapes in the brown, dried leaves of the forest floor and don't find too many. Unfortunately, the fragile ecosystem that supports morels has changed in the last decade in our area. His best picking area has now been paved and made into a bike path. Good for bikers—but bad for morel hunters.

3 tablespoons butter

8 ounces morels

   salt and pepper to taste

Clean morels and slice in half lengthwise. Melt butter in skillet and add mushrooms when it is hot. Sauté until mushrooms release their juices, then reduce heat and cook until liquid evaporates. Season with salt and pepper.

Tips

If you are lucky enough to find a supply of morels, treat them right. Store in a brown paper bag in the vegetable crisper of the refrigerator, taking care not to have too many piled together. That would speed their deterioration.

When ready to use, rinse them carefully to get rid of the tiny bugs that are also fond of morels. Dry the morels carefully before sautéing. Some people like to soak them in saltwater to expel the bugs, but that also leaches out mushroom water (and flavor).

Morels are easy to dry for future use. First wipe them with a soft dry brush or cloth to remove visible dirt. Dry on racks in a gas oven with the pilot light on for 24 hours, or in an electric oven on the lowest possible heat setting with the door open a crack for about 15 hours. Check frequently until they are crisp and completely dry.

Dried mushrooms will last about a year, though they should be checked monthly to be sure they are not infested with bugs that hatch from the eggs of the bugs that are killed during the drying process. If frozen, dried mushrooms will last indefinitely.

Eat the Weeds

Annual Dandelion Salad

SERVES 4

Each year my friend Natalie Thorington, her daughter Natasha, my daughter Rose, and I get together for our annual spring tonic—a feast of dandelion salad. We do it before the lawn has been mowed, while the grass is a riot of shy violets. They bring all the dandelion leaves they can find from their yard, and we gather all we can from our yard, and then fix a salad and have the first dinner of the spring season on the deck. The ritual rejuvenates us and recharges our batteries. The supermarkets have recently been carrying cultivated dandelion greens, but they're not as tender as the ones we gather ourselves for this annual ritual.

4 quarts dandelion greens

4 strips bacon

⅓ cup sugar

2 tablespoons flour

1 teaspoon salt

½ cup apple-cider vinegar

1½ cups water

1 egg, beaten

3 hard-boiled eggs, sliced

violets for garnish

Wash, dry, and cut up tender dandelion greens. Cook bacon over medium-low heat until crisp. Remove bacon from pan, crumble, and reserve. In a medium bowl, combine sugar, flour, and salt. In liquid measure combine vinegar, water, and beaten egg. Pour liquids into dry ingredients and mix until smooth. Pour this mixture into the bacon drippings and heat, whisking constantly until the mixture thickens. Pour hot dressing over the dandelion greens and top with crumbled bacon and slices of hard-boiled egg. Toss lightly and serve immediately, garnished with violets if desired.

Sautéed Fiddleheads

SERVES 2

The forests of Central Pennsylvania often form a high canopy that becomes impenetrable once leaf-out has taken place. In the early spring, when the sun can still penetrate to the forest floor, the fiddlehead ferns emerge, all the potential of their beautiful frond tightly coiled into a Celtic sun symbol. Fiddlehead ferns can be foraged then, and make a nice accompaniment to trout fillet or chicken cutlet, simply prepared. It is important not to overpick fern beds in any one area, because the picked frond will not grow back. Fiddlehead ferns have a very strong, bitter flavor, and a little can go a long way.

1 teaspoon butter

⅓ cup fiddleheads, rinsed and dried

Melt butter in a small sauté pan over medium-high heat. Add the fiddleheads and stir until they turn a bright green color and are tender, about 2 minutes.

Asparagus Season

Sabine Carey and Kim Tait harvest asparagus in the low-riding asparagus buggy.

At Tait Farm, asparagus shares the dark-brown, composted earth with dandelions, groundhogs, and a go-cart-like contraption called the "asparagus buggy." Designed by patriarch Elton Tait, the buggy has two seats that allow convenient riding access to the low-growing crop, hand-harvested by the passengers. The pickers snap and toss asparagus into the plastic flat until every last spear has been gathered. Plant crowns beneath the surface send up more shoots, weather permitting. The plant takes three years to become established and start producing, but will then produce for thirty years.

One of the first vegetables of the new growing season, asparagus is a herald of spring. The plant is native to the Mediterranean region and is said to have sprung from the volcanic ash of Mount Vesuvius in Italy. It was cultivated by the Romans and the Greeks for two hundred years before the birth of Christ. A common Roman expression for timeliness called for doing something "in less time than it takes to cook asparagus."

Asparagus season has become a community event with the Asparagus Festival held at Tait Farm every year. Music, wagon rides, cooking demonstrations, and samplings of various asparagus recipes are held right in the field with the magical asparagus spears shooting up all around. Centre Region residents who don't feel like picking or cooking can patronize the asparagus festival at Mario and Luigi's restaurants, where many dishes, using pasta, polenta, and risotto, provide delicious appreciation of the seasonal delicacy. They can also buy bunches of Tait's asparagus at the restaurant, festively wrapped with ribbon like a bunch of flowers.

Kim Tait's Roasted Asparagus Pâté

SERVES 4 TO 6

- 1 pound asparagus
- 2 tablespoons olive oil
- 2 tablespoons finely minced scallion
- 1 clove garlic, minced
- ⅓ cup Parmesan cheese
- ⅓ cup pine nuts
- ⅛ teaspoon fresh rosemary
- ¼ teaspoon thyme

Preheat oven to 350°F. Arrange asparagus in roasting pan, lightly brush with olive oil, and roast for 12 to 15 minutes, or until just tender. In a small pan, sauté the scallions and garlic in olive oil for a minute or two. Put all the ingredients in a food processor and blend until smooth. Chill for 1 hour. Serve with toast or crackers. Alternatively, spread pâté on slices of Italian bread, sprinkle with Parmesan cheese and pine nuts, and broil until cheese is melted and pine nuts begin to brown.

Tait Farm Asparagus Salsa

- 1 cup cooked asparagus, chopped
- 1 cup tomato, chopped
- ½ cup Vidalia onion, finely chopped
  juice and grated rind of ½ small lime
- ⅓ cup Tait Farm Chipotle Sauce
- 1 small clove of garlic, minced
- ¼ teaspoon salt or to taste
- ⅛ teaspoon cayenne pepper
- ⅛ teaspoon ground cumin
  freshly ground black pepper to taste
  cilantro for garnish

Mix all ingredients together. Allow to sit one hour for flavors to meld. Excellent served with grilled fish, chicken, or tortilla chips.

Memorial Day: A Boalsburg Tradition

The Boalsburg Memorial Day celebration includes a solemn tribute to fallen Pennsylvania soldiers.

The end of the spring marks the beginning of the outdoor cooking season, kicking off with the Memorial Day holiday. Boalsburg holds an annual village-wide celebration to recognize the holiday that began in 1864 when village women decorated the graves of the soldiers killed in the Civil War and laid to rest at the Boalsburg cemetery. In addition to craft sales, music, pie contests, spelling bees, carnival rides for the kids, and Civil War reenactments, most of the town opens its doors to visitors from near and far.

There are lots of eating options in the town, but one of the most interesting is the soup sale at the Harris Township Building on Main Street. Volunteers staff two simmering cauldrons heating over an outdoor wood-fire. The stirrers, who never stop moving, gently rock long poles with paddles at 90° angles. In one of the cauldrons is a "magical" vegetable soup, magical because it is donated by dozens of contributors and everyone uses his or her own recipe! Somehow, the mix is always just right.

The other soup is a bean soup that Wilna Kesler has made for the last ten years. She cooks 24 pounds of beans in three batches and blends them at the site. To accompany the soup, there is bread also donated by the townsfolk. It is a truly cooperative event, by the people, for the people.

Wilna Kesler's Bean Soup

SERVES 8

1 pound dried great northern beans

1 meaty smoked ham bone

3 or more quarts of water

½ to 1 cup chopped onion

½ to 1 cup diced celery

½ to 1 cup diced carrots

   bay leaf

   salt and pepper to taste

Sort the beans, wash, and soak overnight. Cover the ham bone with water in a stockpot and boil until the meat is tender and falling off the bone. Remove 2 tablespoons of ham fat that rises while making the stock, or use oil to sauté the vegetables slightly and then add them to the stockpot. Add the beans and the bay leaf, and make sure there is enough liquid to cover everything by 2 inches. Cook for several hours, with the lid not on too tightly, so that some of the steam escapes. Season with salt and pepper to taste.

Oatmeal Bread

MAKES 2 LOAVES

This is the bread I send to the soup and bread sale on Memorial Day. I don't consider myself a baker, but this is made in the Cuisinart and has been my standard recipe since 1980, when I acquired my first Cuisinart from the Country Sampler in Boalsburg.

Tip

Using a tightly closed plastic container helps the dough to rise more quickly. Also, the dough could be placed in a simulated "proofer" to speed up the rising time: Place the plastic container with dough alongside a pot of hot water in an insulated cooler to bring the temperature up more quickly.

2 teaspoons sugar

2 teaspoons yeast

⅓ cup warm water (110°F)

4 cups unbleached flour

1 cup oats

1 cup whole-wheat flour

2 teaspoons salt

5½ tablespoons cold butter, cut into pieces

1⅔ cups ice water

1 egg, beaten

sprigs of fresh thyme

Place sugar and yeast in liquid measure and stir. Add ⅓ cup warm water. Let stand until foamy, about 5 minutes, to proof the yeast. With the plastic doughhook in place on the Cuisinart, put in unbleached flour, oats, whole-wheat flour, salt, and butter pieces. Process until the butter is cut in and the mixture has the consistency of cornmeal. Add the yeast mixture slowly.

Pour ice water into the liquid measure that held the proofing yeast and measure to 1⅔ cup. Add the ice water in a thin, steady stream and process until the dough is a smooth, round mass. Place the dough in a tightly covered plastic container to rise for about 1 hour, or until doubled.

Punch down and shape into two 1½-pound round loaves and place on parchment-lined baking sheets. Brush the tops of the loaves with beaten egg and place sprigs of fresh thyme on top. Brush herbs with more egg wash to adhere. Cover with plastic wrap that has been sprayed with cooking spray so the herbs don't stick. Preheat oven to 375°F and allow to rise for about 45 minutes, or until doubled in size. Bake for about 25 to 30 minutes, or until golden brown. Cool on wire racks.

Barbecue Time

The Memorial Day holiday also marks the beginning of the outdoor cooking season, when Central Pennsylvanians can be found on decks, porches, lawns, and in the many state parks, with tongs and turners in their hands. Outdoor cooking takes us back to roots we all share, back to an age when small groups of humans huddled around fires impaling cubes of meat on sticks and slowly roasting them until done. Occasionally someone threw a sprig of thyme or cedar into the fire, and suddenly the aroma became more tantalizing.

Civilization tamed the fire to indoor fireplaces, clay ovens, and, later, metal stoves. Cooking methods changed, and the outdoor feast became the province of hunters and fishermen, shepherds, and adventurers. Spanish settlers in the New World found the Caribbean Indians cooking over green-wood grills called barbacoas that were suspended over pits with wood fires. In Virginia, early colonists learned to barbecue pigs in a similar manner.

The term "barbecue" has come to be synonymous with the term "grill," but there are significant differences. Barbecuing is often done in a pit over hardwood or hardwood coals; it is usually a lengthy process. Grilling takes place on a grid over a heat source; it is typically much quicker.

Most grilling requires a bed of coals two inches deep and one or two inches larger in area than the food to be grilled. When the bed of coals is ready, variety wood chips like mesquite that have been soaked previously, or grapevines and bunches of last year's dried herbs, can be added as the food is cooked, to enhance the flavor. This type of grilling is perfectly suited for family dining and small-scale entertaining, when you don't need coals for a long time. For barbecues that last for long periods, charcoal would be more effective, with variety woods like mesquite, hickory, or fruitwoods like cherry or apple added for interest.

Cajun shrimp over a grapevine fire on the grill.

Cook's Note

Charcoal, lump or briquette, is the most common fuel for backyard feasts. Lump charcoal is pure carbonized wood with no additives that lights easily and burns quickly. Charcoal briquettes are a combination of pulverized charcoal held together with cornstarch, with mineral coal added, sodium nitrate to speed ignition, and lime to retard the rate of burning. Briquettes take about forty minutes to produce usable coals; they burn longer but are difficult to light. Charcoal starter—petroleum-based liquid or jelly—helps briquettes start quickly but gives the food an undesirable taste. Gasoline and kerosene are extremely explosive and should never be used to start a fire.

Cajun Seafood Kebabs

SERVES 4

This is my son Joe's favorite grill recipe. A seafood-lover who enjoys spicy foods, Joe tends to these kebabs carefully as they grill.

½ pound shrimp, peeled
   and deveined

½ pound scallops, cleaned
   and connective tissue
   removed

½ pound salmon, cut into
   1-inch cubes

3⅓ tablespoons Homemade
   Cajun Seasoning

1 lemon

Thread seafood, alternating varieties, on bamboo skewers that have been soaked in water for 30 minutes. Coat kebabs thoroughly with seasoning mix. Grill over hot coals for 3 to 5 minutes, turning continually until just cooked. The amount of time will depend on how hot your fire is. Serve with lemon wedges, if desired.

Homemade Cajun Seasoning

Sure, you can buy small bottles of Cajun seasoning at any grocery store today, but look at the prices for just a couple of ounces! This homemade version will save you money in the long run if you purchase the spices in bulk in small bags at a natural foods store or through an herb purveyor. After all, it is just salt and pepper with a few extra seasonings. To make a larger quantity, use a tablespoon or a fractional cup measure and follow the same proportions.

2 teaspoons salt

1 teaspoon black pepper

1 teaspoon white pepper

1 teaspoon cayenne pepper

1 teaspoon paprika

1 teaspoon dried thyme

1 teaspoon dried oregano

1 teaspoon garlic powder

1 teaspoon onion powder

Combine ingredients and store in tightly covered jar. Makes 3⅓ tablespoons.

Tip

To avoid sticking, spray the grill with cooking spray before setting it over the coals.

Summer

Summer *Recipes*

Summer

*S*ummer is the fruitful time in Central Pennsylvania, when the promise of all those seed catalogs is realized. Gardens are prevalent, sprouting from the rich earth, carefully tended, constantly weeded. The landscape is full green now, if the weather has been normal in the spring, with enough rain to fill the streams and lakes and provide an environment for native fishes.

Students and teachers alike kick back and enjoy the luxury of free time. Those who work year-round do so at a less hurried pace in the summer, making time to enjoy the occasional picnic supper at a state park or just in the backyard. The first sound in the morning is the cardinal's song, bright harbinger of the day. Soon all the other birds are up and singing. In the yard, the rabbits hop about in their mating dance while the squirrels regard them, puzzled. The bright, hot days are filled with trips to the pool—a splashy scene that provides the summer social structure for many children. Whipple Dam is our own version of the Riviera, and parents go to lie on the sandy beach while their children splash around, in the protected waters.

Those who prefer quiet head to the woods and find a stream for wading. If they are lucky, they know of a secret swimming hole where submersion in the cool, dark water brings instant relief from *the heat. Just being in the woods is a vacation—the scent of the hemlock and pine, the soft cushion of moss, and maybe a mushroom or two. The summer mushrooms, dependent on rain, can provide a feast when toted home and prepared with care.*

The days are long, and the evenings stretch out, filled with baseball games and tennis matches, badminton and long walks with neighborhood friends. When the dark finally does overcome, it is lit with the flicker of fireflies, Pennsylvania's state insect, and their capture and release provide entertainment until bedtime.

Father's Day, in mid-June, provides a good excuse for a cookout, particularly if you can cook something Dad hunted or fished for himself. Trout and venison, both excellent prepared on the grill, satisfy in a fundamental way, a testament to the bounty of the region. A semi-professional baseball game is a good way to spend time with Dad and to check out the stadium in Altoona that is home to the Altoona Curve.

Midsummer is a time to delight in all the gifts of the land, and sometimes it's hard to fit all the meals in. Eating from the garden becomes the regional pastime, and those without gardens can frequent the many excellent farmers' markets. Rhubarb starts the inundation that seems to accelerate weekly, through strawberries, blueberries, raspberries, cherries, peaches, zucchini, beans, eggplant, peppers—and the two home-grown favorites, corn and tomatoes. Tomatoes ripe from the garden are perfect at every meal, on one of Irving's bagels spread with cream cheese in the morning, tucked into a sandwich at lunch, and on grilled Italian bread for bruschetta at dinner. Tomatoes are the reason most gardeners go through the effort of gardening, and the taste of a home-grown tomato never disappoints.

The Central Pennsylvania Festival of the Arts, or Arts Festival, quickens the pace of the Centre Region in July, when tens of thousands of people come to celebrate the visual and performing arts. The crowds of artists and shoppers alike are interesting in themselves, and the outdoor cafés provide excellent posts for people-watching. Boalsburg concurrently offers the People's Choice Festival, which features many crafts that celebrate a country style.

August brings a slowdown, as many people leave town for one last trip before the frenetic pace of fall kicks in. The days are quiet, the gardens are full; canning season is upon us. Soon there is a familiar wake-up call on our roof—thud, roll, roll, roll—the apples are coming, the apples are coming. Squirrels and rabbits alike perch in the lawn, tiny paws gripping small fallen apples.

The Grange Fair takes place at the end of the summer, just before the children return to school. A farmers' festival, it is the largest tent encampment of its type left in the nation. A trip to the Grange Fair is part of the cycle of the year and is not to be forgotten. Celebrating the largesse of the land as well as the farmers' noble efforts, it keeps us all in tune with our roots.

The halcyon days of late summer are over. At the end of August, arrival day delivers tens of thousands of students to buzzing dorms and apartments. State College and the Penn State campus become a snarl of parked cars with flashing lights depositing students and massive piles of belongings. The pace all over town quickens, and an electricity of expectation and excitement fills the air. Parents escorting offspring to the brink of a new era marks not only the beginning of our yearly cycle here but also, in a larger sense, a turning of the generational wheel that so many of us are a part of here in Central Pennsylvania.

A great swelling pops buttons of berries
near a field alert with corn.
Deacon trees, fulfilled with green leaves,
Bless the bounty of earth adorned.

Father's Day

Central Pennsylvania often serves as a proving ground for chefs fresh from culinary school before they move on to metropolitan areas. The clientele of area hotels and restaurants have adventurous palates and will support the flights of fancy of a creative chef. The tenure of Brendan McGovern at the Atherton Hotel was one that proved beneficial to the community. A graduate of the Baltimore International Culinary College, Brendan kept his creative juices flowing by serving special "chef's tables," prearranged dinners that gave him the freedom to choose the menu based on seasonal availability. Also, he frequently gave cooking classes in the commercial kitchen at the hotel, including one for Father's Day geared for children. At this class in 1997 brothers Kyle and Brendyn Dornich learned how to create a meal for the family. Brendan, a native of Philadelphia and the youngest of seven children, enjoys cooking Plum Barbecued Chicken for his own father.

Kyle and Brendyn Dornich get a cooking lesson from Brendan McGovern.

Brendan McGovern's Plum Barbecued Chicken

SERVES 6 TO 8

1 tablespoon extra-virgin olive oil

1 Spanish onion, chopped

¼ stalk celery, chopped

2 cloves garlic, chopped

1 habanero chili pepper, seeded and chopped

2 plums, seeded and chopped

2 tomatoes, seeded and chopped

1 cup red-wine vinegar

2 tablespoons molasses

¼ cup brewed Irish tea

2 whole chickens, cut into eight pieces each

salt and pepper

Heat olive oil and sauté onion, celery, garlic, and chili pepper until translucent. Add plums and tomatoes and continue cooking for an additional 5 minutes. Add vinegar, molasses, and tea and simmer for 45 minutes. Puree until smooth in food processor or blender. Season with salt and pepper to taste.

Reserve ⅔ cup of the marinade and dredge chicken pieces with the remaining marinade. Grill chicken over hot coals for 30 to 45 minutes, basting occasionally with the marinade. Cook until the juices run clear when the meat is pierced with a fork. Near the end of the cooking time, brush with the reserved marinade.

Tip

When seeding hot peppers, disposable plastic gloves will protect your fingers from the burning sensation due to the capsaicin, the oil produced by glands at the junction of the ribs and the interior wall. Habanero peppers, also known as Scotch bonnets, are the hottest of all the pepper varieties.

Warning

Be sure to thoroughly cook any marinade that came in contact with the raw chicken, to avoid the risk of salmonella.

Debra Fasick preserves
fish by smoking.

How about honoring Dad by making him a special treat with some of his hard-won prizes from local streams—namely, his prize trout?

The entire Fasick family participated when eldest daughter Debra ran her fish market, the Seafood Centre, from 1982 to 1986 on South Atherton Street in State College. Mother Rose worked in the shop along with Debbie and her sister Pam. Every week, Debbie drove a large van down to the docks in Baltimore, Maryland, for the wide variety of seafood available there. Whatever fish didn't sell was smoked by a method that Debbie learned from her father, Eugene, who converted an old commercial refrigerator into a smoker by placing a hibachi on the bottom and hanging some hooks from the top. Five metal racks allowed plenty of surface area for laying out the fish. Eugene gathered hickory from the surrounding forest because it burns slowly and imparts a good flavor, though any other fruitwood—apple, cherry, or peach—could be used.

At home, a covered kettle grill can serve as a smoker if both top and bottom vents are left open to allow a draft to circulate. The intensity of the fire is critical to the procedure. The fire must be smoldering—never flaming, which demands constant attention. Debbie used a propane torch to light the fire, instead of newspapers that create a dirty ash. Also, she kept a piece of sheet metal over the fire to create more smoke. Eventually, her smoked fish became so popular that she was ordering far more of the fresh than she could sell to keep up with the demand for the smoked variety. And she was hauling some of her smoked product back down to Baltimore for her purveyors to enjoy.

Debra Fasick's
Smoked Fish with Mustard Dill Sauce

MAKES 16 TWO-OUNCE SERVINGS

Well-wrapped and refrigerated, smoked fish will keep for about two weeks because of the salting. It also can be frozen, so it is a good idea to do a large batch at one time—when you can afford the time. Mustard Dill Sauce is a nice counterpoint to the robust flavor of smoked tuna, bluefish, and salmon.

2 pounds fish for smoking (trout, salmon, bluefish, whitefish, tuna—any available variety)

BRINE FOR SOAKING:

2 quarts water

½ cup brown sugar

½ cup kosher salt

Mustard Dill Sauce

Combine water, brown sugar, and salt. Soak fish in a single layer in the brine overnight in the refrigerator. The fish must be completely covered by the solution. When you are ready to smoke, remove fish and air-dry on a rack until there is no more dripping, about 30 minutes.

Prepare a hickory, fruitwood, or mesquite fire in a kettle smoker, and leave the vents open so it does not burn too hot. Replenish wood supply as needed to keep the smoke going. Arrange fish on the rack, with the largest pieces closest to the heat source. Have water at hand in a spray bottle to squirt the fire if it bursts into flame.

Fillets, salmon and tuna steaks, and boned and butterflied trout will take about 3 hours to smoke. The fish should be firm to the touch and golden brown, cooked but still moist inside. Just as with regular fish cookery, it is ready when it is opaque all the way through. Serve with Mustard Dill Sauce.

Mustard Dill Sauce

4 tablespoons Pommery mustard (or other dark, whole-seed mustard)

1 teaspoon ground mustard powder

4 teaspoons sugar

2 tablespoons white vinegar

⅓ cup olive oil

3 tablespoons fresh dill, chopped

In a small, deep bowl, mix the wet and dry mustards together, then add the sugar and vinegar. With a wire whisk, slowly beat in the oil until the mixture forms a thick emulsion. Stir in the chopped dill. Makes ¾ cup.

Tip

Kosher salt is preferred by chefs because it is a purer form of salt, without any additives. The larger, square grains have more flavor than table salt, which is finely ground. Because of the grind, table salt is denser than kosher salt, and 1 tablespoon of table salt contains 25 percent more salt than sea salt and 50 percent more salt than kosher salt, which has a fluffy texture.

Summer's Bounty : Rhubarb

*Early summer is rhubarb season in Central Pennsylvania, and few people who have tried rhubarb are uncommitted about whether they love or hate this conundrum of a vegetable that acts as a fruit. Garden rhubarb—*Rheum rhaponticum, *or pie plant, as it is commonly called—is a cool-climate perennial of the buckwheat family. Native to southern Siberia and the Volga region, rhubarb has been cultivated for centuries in Asian countries before being introduced to Europe around A.D. 1600. By 1800, horticulturists in America were listing its varieties.*

Rhubarb's large, red-veined leaves spring from a crown several inches beneath the soil, under which a deep network of roots penetrates several feet into the earth. Some of the roots are enlarged to store food for the early spring growth of the plant. The edible portion of the plant is the thick, reddish leaf stalk. The leaves themselves are poisonous due to a high concentration of oxalic acid, which could be fatal if ingested. Rhubarb is typically made into pies, but it also makes a restorative tonic when cooked in a little water (1 pound rhubarb to 2 cups water) for 10 minutes, strained, then sweetened to taste.

Rhubarb Crisp

SERVES 6

Rhubarb Crisp is an easy and nutritious way to use this unusual plant.

Tip

There are several ways to cut butter or other fat into a dry mix. Two knives will suffice: move them crisscross against each other rapidly. A pastry blender, a semicircle of wire comb with a handle, is more efficient. The food processor is my personal favorite method because only a couple of pulses will result in a crumb of perfect consistency with the butter well dispersed.

1 cup oatmeal
½ cup flour
1 cup brown sugar
½ cup butter

3 cups rhubarb, diced and mixed with:
½ cup sugar
1 teaspoon cinnamon
pinch of salt
1 tablespoon water
optional: vanilla ice cream or heavy cream

Preheat oven to 350°F. Butter or spray an 8-inch-square baking pan. Mix oats, flour, and brown sugar together and cut in butter until mixture is uniformly crumbly. Place half the crumb mixture in the pan. Prepare rhubarb mixture and place on top. Sprinkle with remaining crumb mixture. Bake for 45 minutes. Cut into squares and serve hot or warm with ice cream or heavy cream, if desired.

Sue Smith's Rhubarb Cake

SERVES 12

Sue Smith and her husband, Ron, live in Lemont and are active members of the community, visible through volunteer efforts in many arenas. Sue has served as chairman of the Family Health Services advisory committee and chaired the Interfaith Mission, which is made up of thirty-eight different congregations. She hits the streets in December, overseeing the Salvation Army kettle drive. Sue is also a frequent contributor to the editorial page, drawing attention to issues over a wide range of subjects. She is one of the voices of our community. Professionally, she works as a consultant for nonprofit groups, giving advice on fundraising and development.

Sue has taken this cake to potlucks and received many compliments on it, the most notable from a five-year-old girl who asked what it was, and who, when Sue told her, protested, saying, "It can't be rhubarb! It's too good!"

1½ cups brown sugar

½ cup olive oil

1 large egg

2 cups sifted flour

1 cup sour milk with 1 teaspoon baking soda mixed in

1 teaspoon vanilla

1½ cups chopped rhubarb

2 teaspoons sugar

1 teaspoon cinnamon

Preheat oven to 350°F. Prepare a 9 x 13 inch pan by spraying it with cooking spray or greasing. Put brown sugar, olive oil, and egg in the bowl of an electric mixer and cream together. Alternately add the sifted flour along with the sour milk–baking soda mixture, using one-third of each at a time. Beat in the vanilla and the rhubarb. Spread in the prepared pan. Combine the sugar and the cinnamon and sprinkle over the top. Bake for 40 to 50 minutes, until an inserted cake tester or toothpick comes out clean.

Cook's Note

Olive oil labeled "extra virgin" and "cold-pressed" is the finest and most expensive of the olive oils. It has a deep green color and a pronounced olive flavor that make it perfect for using on salads or on bread as a dipping oil. Golden olive oils result from subsequent extractions that usually employ heat. There are fewer olive solids in these types and, subsequently, less olive color and flavor. Relative to other oils, olive oil has a low smoke point (375°F), which is the temperature at which it begins to break down chemically into acrolein, a substance that irritates the eyes and nose.

Fourth of July at Centre Furnace Mansion

Deanna Nardozza, dressed in Victorian garb, greets visitors at Centre Furnace Mansion.

Centre Furnace Mansion, headquarters of the Centre County Historical Society, is one of the true gems of the Centre Region. The Mansion was the ironmaster's residence for Centre Furnace, the first charcoal iron furnace in Centre County, and was the birthplace of the Pennsylvania State University. Heroically rescued in 1978 from private ownership that chopped the stately building into student apartments, the mansion is continually improving, thanks to a core of dedicated volunteers spear-headed by Jackie Melander, president of the historical society. It is furnished to reflect the period of residency of ironmaster Moses Thompson, 1842–1891, and his family.

The busy social calendar of the historical society attests to the out-reach efforts of the members. There is always something going on at the Mansion—exhibits, lectures, forums, receptions, plant sales, meetings, and old-fashioned community events like their annual Fourth of July picnic. Inaugurated in 1982, the Old-Fashioned Independence Day celebration commences at high noon and is carried on in a Victorian tradition. The ringing of the Centre Furnace bell, which was forged on the site in the early 1800s, calls the crowd to order. Fife music accompanies the raising of the flag, and the powerful words of the Declaration of Independence stir the multitude, who know full well the cost of those freedoms we hold so dear.

Afterward, the party begins with a Victorian picnic on the lawn. Attendees are invited to bring a favorite main dish or salad to share and are encouraged to bring old family recipes to showcase the diversity of our ethnic heritage. The following recipe is from the files of Anna Elliott Thompson, one of the original residents of the mansion.

Anna Elliott Thompson's Superior Gingerbread

SERVES 12

4 cups flour

1 cup sugar

1 teaspoon baking soda

2 teaspoons powdered ginger

2 teaspoons cinnamon

1 teaspoon ground cloves

1 cup butter

3 eggs

1 cup molasses

1 cup boiling water

powdered sugar, for garnish

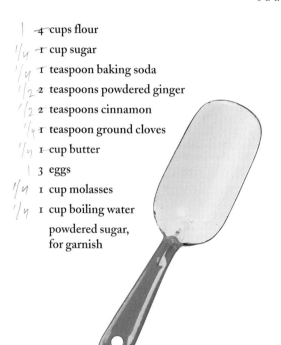

Preheat oven to 350°F. Prepare a 9 x 13 inch baking pan with cooking spray or by greasing and flouring. Combine dry ingredients in a large bowl, then cut in butter. Combine the eggs and the molasses, add the dry ingredients, then add the boiling water and mix, using as few strokes as possible. Bake for 45 to 50 minutes, until the gingerbread tests done with a toothpick. Sprinkle with powdered sugar, if desired, when it is cool.

Tip

Whole spices that are freshly ground in a coffee grinder reserved for that purpose are much better in cooking because the volatile oils lend far more flavor than most ready-ground spices. A mini blender attachment can also be used.

Summer's Bounty : Zucchini

Scott Case and Charlie Boyer sell home-grown produce to Sandy Lindenbaum.

The rich soil of Pennsylvania yields a prodigious bounty in the summer. Produce stands dot country roads, and anyone with too much zucchini in the garden sets a card table at the end of the lane, stacks the squash like cordwood according to size, and sets a coffee can out to collect the money.

Farmers' markets are plentiful in Central Pennsylvania in the summertime, with one open in the Centre Region nearly every day of the week. This arena provides the perfect place for dialogue between producer and consumer. Most farmers are happy to chat about the methods they use to grow their favorite varieties, and bask in the consumer's one-on-one appreciation. Subscription gardens, whose patrons prepay for a season's worth of produce, are also getting more popular in the area as local consumers too busy to garden on their own desire more control over their food source.

Two longtime purveyors illustrate very different base operations. Scott Case and his wife, Eda, have been farming for nine years on land that was previously farmed by Eda's parents, Jeanne and Bob McCarthy. Theirs is a certified organic farm with a large greenhouse and five acres in production. Depending on the time of year, they employ between two and twelve people from the surrounding Penns Valley area.

Emma Wance's Zucchini Bread

MAKES 2 LOAVES

Emma Wance, from Aaronsburg, picks and brings the vegetables she raises in her own home garden to both the State College and the Boalsburg markets. She also bakes, specializing in zucchini bread to use up some of her abundant squash supply. This recipe has withstood the test of time. She cut it out of the Centre Daily Times *on August 27, 1975, and has used it continually ever since. The dog-eared clipping, yellowed and coated with two decades of flour dust and batter splashes, is the mainstay of her offerings and has a devoted following.*

Emma Wance's popular Zucchini Bread.

3 eggs

1 cup oil

2 cups brown sugar

2 cups zucchini, grated

1 tablespoon vanilla

3 cups flour

1 teaspoon salt

1 teaspoon baking soda

1 teaspoon baking powder

1 tablespoon cinnamon

1 cup chopped walnuts

Preheat oven to 325°F. Spray two 9 x 5 x 3 inch loaf pans with cooking spray, or grease lightly. Beat eggs, add oil, brown sugar, zucchini, and vanilla. Combine dry ingredients and make a well in the center. Add wet ingredients to the dry ingredients and combine. Divide mixture between the two prepared pans. Bake for 1 hour, or until toothpick inserted in loaf comes out clean.

Tip

Use a kitchen scale to be sure that you pour the same amount of batter into each pan.

Cook's Note

Walnuts are native to Asia, Europe, and North America. The black walnut is the major American species and comes from the Appalachian region. English walnuts, which originated in Europe, are now grown primarily in California. Much easier to shell than black walnuts, producers prefer them. Emma Wance uses a mixture of English walnuts and black walnuts.

Here are two other zucchini recipes that are quick and easy, which zucchini recipes need to be so you can quickly use up the day's harvest of the prolific vegetable.

Cook's Note

Summer squash are in the same family as winter squash, **Cucurbita pepo,** *but the summer varieties are harvested when they are immature. Both summer and winter squashes are gourds—fleshy vegetables with seeds on the inside and protective rinds outside. One way to reduce zucchini production is to pick the flowers when they emerge, stuff them with a meat or cheese filling, and coat with a light batter (see Roger Fisher's Flower Tempura, page 12) and fry. Another way to keep zucchini in check is to harvest them young, from barely more than finger-size to no larger than 8 inches long. All squash should be picked when at the edible stage whether it can be used or not, in order to keep the vines bearing well. When a few are permitted to grow very large and to mature, production will slow down or stop altogether. Summer squash that is allowed to mature has leathery skin and seeds that are large and tough, and suffers a loss of flavor.*

Sautéed Zucchini

SERVES 6

This recipe is adapted from a deck of large playing cards that had perfect French recipes on them. My husband received the cards from his parents in 1969, and we still use this recipe all the time.

- 3 tablespoons olive oil
- 2 cloves garlic, finely chopped
- 6 small or 3 medium zucchini, cut into ½-inch slices
- 1 teaspoon oregano
  salt and freshly ground pepper
- 2 tablespoons parsley, finely chopped

Heat olive oil in heavy skillet and add garlic. Sauté for a minute or two, taking care not to let the garlic get brown. Add zucchini slices and toss to coat with the flavored oil. Continue to cook for 5 minutes, stirring, or until the zucchini is tender, slightly brown, and still firm. Add oregano, and season with salt and freshly ground pepper. Serve sprinkled with parsley.

Zucchini Milano

SERVES 6

My son Alex calls this "zucchini pizza," and it is one of his favorites. This dish can also be made with peeled, quartered, thinly sliced eggplant.

- 6 small or 3 medium zucchini, cut into ½-inch slices
- 15 ounces tomato sauce
- 1 cup shredded cheddar cheese
- ¼ teaspoon dried basil or oregano

Heat oven to 350°F. Spray a large casserole dish with baking spray and arrange the zucchini in a single layer, shingled. Pour tomato sauce over the squash and top with cheese and basil or oregano. Cover with foil and bake for about 30 minutes. Remove foil after 30 minutes, then continue to bake for an additional 15 minutes, or until zucchini tests tender.

Summer's Bounty : Herbs

Susan and Rob Haney have hewn a home and a livelihood in the hills near Coburn in Penns Valley. Two acres of the 6½-acre property are devoted to gardens where Susan grows herbs and flowers that she sells at the State College farmers' market on Fridays during the summer. Her husband works in wood and has crafted a charming residence for them and their two children, Carston and Greta, in the former milkhouse adjoining a cavernous 1840s-era barn that houses his woodworking operation and the workshop for her floral creations.

A stroll through Susan's orderly and unfenced garden beds shows her ability to connect with and harness the power of her own piece of Pennsylvania. Her gardens have an architectural order and symmetry that both stimulate and soothe. Tall blue delphiniums stand guard over rows of basil, artichoke bristles next to deep burgundy amaranth, and bright-green parsley contrasts with the smooth blue of the onion stems as the profusion emerges from the rich brown soil.

The Haneys live in harmony with their environment. "The farmers' market provides a balance for me, a day chock-full of folks chatting and exchanging greetings, information, and money for goods," said Susan. "The rest of the week is busy also, but peaceful. And Rob and I take a few moments daily to stand where we live, look around us, and give thanks for this bit of land, for good neighbors, for health, for the miracle of being able to produce so much from those little packs of seeds."

Sue Haney arranges her sunflowers at the farmers' market.

Sue Haney's Lemon-Garlic Dressing for Green Salad

MAKES ABOUT 1 CUP

- 4 tablespoons fresh lemon juice
- 1 teaspoon lemon zest
- 2 large cloves garlic, minced
- ⅔ cup extra-virgin olive oil

  salt and pepper

Combine the lemon juice, lemon zest, and garlic, then slowly whisk in the olive oil. Season to taste with salt and pepper.

Sue Haney's Basil Pesto

MAKES ABOUT 1 CUP

- 4 large garlic cloves
- 2 cups fresh basil leaves (without stems or water)
- ½ cup extra-virgin olive oil

  salt and pepper
- ¼ cup pine nuts or walnuts (optional)
- ¼ cup good-quality Parmesan cheese (optional)

Place garlic in food processor and mince. Add basil, turn on processor, and slowly pour olive oil through the tube, continuing to process until all is a puree. Season to taste with salt and pepper and add optional ingredients if desired. Pesto is best eaten when freshly made, but it can be stored in the refrigerator for a week or so and can be frozen for out-of-season meals.

Tip

This tip is from Dorothy Blair, a professor in the nutrition department at Penn State who grows most of her own vegetable supply, preserving what she can for the winter months. To store a large amount of basil when it is abundant and inexpensive in the summer months for use throughout the year, puree it with olive oil in a food processor. Add the garlic, cheese, nuts, and seasonings when you are ready to enjoy it, and the pesto will taste fresher. Also, it will not take up as much room in the freezer, and those additional items are usually on hand. The pureed basil can be frozen in ice-cube trays until solid and then be stored in a plastic bag for quick addition to soups and stews as well as ingredients for the traditional topping for pasta.

Summer's Bounty : Berries and Cherries

The smell of strawberries triggers memories of summer as sweet and welcome as the first warm day. From the genus Fragaria, *whose Latin root also gives us the word "fragrant," the plant has more than twenty species, though only a few are important commercially.* F. vesca, *the wood of Alpine berry, is from Europe;* F. chiloensis *is native to the Pacific Coast; and* F. virginiana *is the eastern American wild strawberry. Strawberries have been in home gardens only since 1830, when seedlings were developed near Boston. Highly prized, for centuries they were available only in the wild. Their scarcity led to high demand and high prices. At one time in England they could fetch prices of 10 pounds sterling for one pound of berries—and their delivery was threatened by highway robbers filled with strawberry greed and not willing to stoop in the wilds and pick them one by one.*

Mid-June is strawberry season in Central Pennsylvania. Strawberry festivals abound, many staged by area churches. One is put on by an entire village to celebrate the glories of the first sweet berry of the summer season. Lemont, at the foot of Mount Nittany, has held an annual strawberry festival since 1980 to benefit the village association. For years the event was held in the parking lot of the post office, but recently it has moved to the village green near the old granary building that is under renovation. A dozen volunteers prepare the berries the night before the Saturday evening event, hulling 128 quarts for the 450 people who attend. Organizer Sue Smith says that bakers in the community donate cakes to accompany the berries. Traditional biscuit-type shortcake, angel food, sponge cake, and chocolate are among the most popular varieties. Meyer's Dairy ice cream is also served. "We used to pick the berries for the festival," Sue says, "but nowadays we buy them from Harner's. Just hulling them is enough of a job!"

Pick-your-own strawberry farms are popular for enthusiasts who don't grow their own. Farm stands and farmers' markets are other good sources for the local fruit, which is so much sweeter and more flavorful than the supermarket variety.

Sara Pitzer's Strawberry Shortcake

SERVES 6

Former Centre County journalist Sara Pitzer has written a cookbook, Simply Strawberries *(Garden Way Publishing, 1985), devoted entirely to strawberries and containing more than one hundred recipes ranging from soups, salads, and entrées to desserts. This is one of her two recipes for Strawberry Shortcake.*

7½ cups sliced strawberries

½ cup granulated sugar

1 cup whole strawberries

2 cups all-purpose, unbleached white flour

1 tablespoon baking powder

1 tablespoon granulated sugar

½ teaspoon salt

¼ cup butter

2 eggs

⅓ cup light cream

¼ cup butter, softened

¾ cup heavy cream

First make the filling: Mash the sliced strawberries lightly with a fork as you stir in the sugar. Refrigerate for at least 1 hour to draw out the juice and dissolve the sugar. Wash, hull, and drain the whole strawberries. Hold until serving time.

Preheat oven to 425°F. Stir together the flour, baking powder, sugar, and salt. Cut in the butter using a pastry blender or two knives until it is like small peas in the flour. Make a well in the center. Beat the eggs. Combine the beaten eggs and light cream and pour into the well in the flour. Mix the dough lightly, as you would for biscuits, just long enough to make the dough hold together.

On a lightly floured surface, pat the dough to about ½ inch thick. Use a biscuit cutter or large inverted glass to cut six individual cakes. Gather up the scraps to form an extra cake for anyone who wants seconds. Place the cakes on a lightly greased or parchment-lined cookie sheet and bake in the preheated oven for 10 to 15 minutes, or until brown.

At serving time, stir the whole berries into the chilled, sugared berries. Split the shortcakes while they are hot, spread with softened butter, and fill and cover with the strawberry filling. This kind of shortcake is traditionally served with heavy cream passed in a pitcher to pour over each serving.

Blueberries are another popular local berry in the summer. Wild blueberries, smaller and more intensely flavored than cultivated varieties, can be gathered in the woods starting in early to mid-July.

The term "blueberry" includes several species of the genus Vaccinium *with a long list of hybridized varieties.* V. angustifolium *is the wild, low-bush "blue" of New England and eastern Canada.* V. corymbosum *is a high-bush variety that is the most popular for cultivation. Huckleberries, also widely available in the fields and forests of Central Pennsylvania, are often confused with blueberries but actually belong to the genus* Gaylussacia, *which is the heath family. Although the fruit is similar, huckleberries have ten tiny hard seeds, while blueberries have soft seeds that are virtually unnoticeable.*

Blueberry Blintzes

SERVES 4

- 8 ounces cream cheese
- 8 ounces ricotta cheese
- ¼ cup sugar
- 12 basic crepes, from your favorite recipe or purchased
- 2 tablespoons butter, melted
- 4 tablespoons sour cream (optional)
  Blueberry Sauce

Beat together cream cheese, ricotta cheese, and sugar until smooth. To assemble each blintz, place about 2 tablespoons of cheese filling at the center of the crepe. Fold sides over filling, then fold bottom and top toward center. Place flap-side down on a serving platter or ovenproof casserole dish, if you want to hold them in the oven. Brush filled blintzes with melted butter. Serve with warm Blueberry Sauce and garnish with sour cream, if desired.

Blueberry Sauce

- 1½ cups cold water
- 2 tablespoons cornstarch
- 2 cups blueberries, fresh or frozen
- ¼ cup sugar

Make a slurry by whisking together ¼ cup water and the cornstarch. Combine remaining 1¼ cups water, the blueberries, and the sugar in a small saucepan. Bring quickly to a boil. Add the slurry and reduce heat, stirring constantly until thickened. Serve warm.

Cook's Notes

Selecting: At the market, look for firm, plump blueberries with an attractive blue-gray "bloom"—the natural waxy coating that varies in shade with the variety. When picking in the wild, keep your eye on the berries. From the point the berries turn blue, the fruit needs another week on the vine to reach absolute ripeness and sweetness. Once home, refrigerate at once, and they will keep for up to three weeks. Don't rinse until you are ready to use them.

Freezing: To freeze, rinse berries, roll them in towels to blot excess moisture, and spread them in one layer on jelly-roll pans until marble-hard. Store, labeled and dated, in freezer bags or containers, removing as much air from the containers as possible.

Fact: Native Americans used to gather and dry blueberries for use in the winter. Pilgrims welcomed them as a substitute for hard-to-get imported raisins and currants.

Pam Harner's Blueberry Pie

MAKES ONE 9- OR 10-INCH PIE

Harner Farm, at the corner of Whitehall Road and West College Avenue, is appealing for a lot of reasons, not the least of which are the wonderful pies Pam Harner bakes and sells there. The aroma is irresistible if you go on baking day, generally Friday mornings, when it's likely that thirty or so pies—apple, peach, and blueberry—are going in and out of the ovens.

unbaked pastry crust for one-crust pie

5 cups fresh or frozen blueberries
(if using frozen berries, allow to
stand for 15 to 30 minutes)

¾ cup sugar

⅓ cup flour

2 teaspoons lemon zest

1 tablespoon lemon juice

CRUMB TOPPING:

½ cup sugar

¾ cup flour

1 teaspoon cinnamon

⅓ cup butter or margarine

Preheat oven to 375°F. Combine the blueberries, sugar, flour, lemon zest and lemon juice and mix. In a separate bowl for the Crumb Topping, combine the sugar, flour and cinnamon and cut in the butter with pastry blender, food processor, or your fingers until you have coarse crumbs. Put the crumb mixture on top of the fruit. Bake for about 45 minutes, until the top is nicely browned and the fruit is bubbling.

Tips

A pastry cloth and a pastry sock that slips over the rolling pin guarantee a tender crust, because you won't have to add too much flour to the surface to prevent sticking.

Pastry guides are wooden sticks that come ¼ inch thick (for pies) and ½ inch thick (for biscuits), so you can keep all your dough the same height and achieve a professional-looking finished product.

Parchment paper can be used to line baking trays so you won't have to grease or spray the baking surface. Your products won't stick, and cleanup will be a breeze.

Blueberry Muffins

MAKES 12

During the first year of operation for the former Encore bookstore in State College, Barbara Lange and I were partners in Q's Café, an espresso bar located there. Every morning we met at 6 A.M. in my catering kitchen and baked a new muffin for the day, along with many other baked goods and savory specials. This blueberry variety was the favorite. It is a low-fat version that we varied with many other types of fruit, depending on what was at hand.

1 egg

½ cup skim milk

½ cup nonfat vanilla yogurt

3 tablespoons oil

2 cups unbleached flour

½ cup sugar

4 teaspoons baking powder

½ teaspoon salt

1½ cups blueberries, fresh or frozen

TOPPING:

3 tablespoons sugar

2 tablespoons walnuts, finely chopped

¼ teaspoon cinnamon

Preheat oven to 400°F. Spray a muffin tin with nonstick cooking spray. In a small bowl, whisk together the egg, milk, yogurt, and oil. Combine flour, sugar, baking powder, and salt in a larger bowl, make a well in the center, and add the liquid to the dry ingredients. Stir the batter just enough to blend and fold in the blueberries. Do not overbeat.

Fill the prepared muffin tin with the batter so that each cup is two-thirds full. Combine topping ingredients in a small bowl and sprinkle over the top of each. Bake for about 20 minutes, or until golden brown.

Raspberry season rolls in right after blueberry season in our area, keeping all the berry-pickers busy, with red and blue stains on their fingertips. Cousin to the rose and the sturdy blackberry, this elegant bramble fruit is from the genus Rubus. *Red raspberries are* R. strigosus; *black raspberries, also called black caps, are* R. occidentalis. *A cross between the two has produced a purple species,* R. neglectus. *Yellow and white varieties are mutations of the red—interesting as novelties, but lacking the essential flavor of the red varieties.*

Raspberries are highly perishable and in peak condition will keep for two days at most. This is why they are so scarce at the supermarkets and always expensive. The best way to acquire them is to pick them yourself, in the wild if you can find a spot, or at a you-pick farm. Ideally, raspberries are best eaten at the moment of harvest, popped into the mouth and pressed against the roof of the mouth with the tongue. Chilling dulls the flavor.

At home, refrigerate the berries as is or spread them in a single layer on a large plate. If you plan to serve them with sugar, use superfine and sprinkle it on them about 15 minutes before you plan to use them. Remove berries from the refrigerator an hour before serving so they can release their full flavor.

True devotees prefer their berries unwashed because contact with water causes rapid deterioration. If you do intend to wash them, don't use running water. Instead, drop them a few at a time into a bowl of cold water and lift out gently with a slotted spoon to drain on paper towels. Handle with care—they deserve it.

Raspberry Corn Muffins

MAKES 12

Lighter than the typical corn muffin, these muffins still have all the down-home character-istics of that American classic. The addition of raspberries makes them very special.

        2 eggs

        1 cup milk

        1 teaspoon vanilla

    1½ cups all-purpose flour

        ¾ cup sugar

        ¾ cup yellow cornmeal

        2 teaspoons baking powder

        ½ teaspoon salt

    1½ cups fresh raspberries

        4 tablespoons unsalted butter, melted

Preheat oven to 400°F. Spray or lightly grease 12 muffin cups, 2½ inches in diameter. In a medium bowl, beat the eggs, milk, and vanilla together until frothy. In a large bowl, stir together the flour, sugar, cornmeal, baking powder, and salt. With the back of a spoon, make a well in the center of the dry mixture. In a small bowl, gently toss the raspberries with 2 tablespoons of the flour mixture until lightly coated. Pour the egg-milk mixture and the melted butter into the remaining flour mixture. Stir quickly, with just 10 or 15 strokes to blend; the batter will be slightly lumpy.

Spoon about 2 tablespoons of batter into each prepared muffin cup. Working quickly, scatter six or eight floured raspberries in each cup. Spoon the remaining batter over the top of each of the muffins, dividing equally. Bake for about 15 minutes, or until the muffins are golden brown and a toothpick inserted in the center comes out clean.

Cook's Notes

Selecting: Dull, lackluster rasp-berries are over the hill. Overripe berries sink in the container. Inspect the bottoms of the containers for moisture stains, which indicate that the berries have been squashed or have molded. A few moldy berries will taint the flavor of the entire basket.

Freezing: Raspberries freeze very well and will keep for a year at 0°F or less. For individual frozen berries, spread raspberries in a single layer on jelly-roll pans, and place in freezer until hard, usually 1 or 2 hours. Transfer the fruit to rigid freezer containers or heavy-duty freezer bags. If it doesn't matter if they all stick together, berries can also be frozen directly in freezer containers, with or without sugar or syrup. To freeze with sugar, use ¾ cup superfine sugar to 1 quart of berries, stirring the berries gently on a wide platter. Let stand until sugar partly dissolves, then pack. To freeze with syrup, use a solution of 2½ cups sugar to each 2 cups chilled water. Pack berries in con-tainers, cover with the syrup, cover with lid, label, date, and freeze.

East of Boalsburg on U.S. Route 322, Tait Farm graces the slope of Tussey Ridge opposite Mount Nittany and yields a variety of crops that keep the entire Tait family busy year-round. In the spring it's rhubarb, then asparagus; in summer, a fabulous crop of raspberries. The cool, crisp weather of fall ripens the apples, and in winter there are varieties of pine and spruce for Christmas trees. Periodically, litters of basset hound puppies draw the attention of the customers at Tait's roadside Harvest Shop. Shoppers frequently go home with far more than the herb plants or gift baskets they came for.

The signature item at the farm, created in 1982, is "Raspberry Shrub," an old-fashioned elixir with remarkable thirst-quenching properties when mixed with sparkling water. A 1986 bumper crop of black raspberries inspired the late David Tait to mass-produce the family favorite and market it as a gourmet item. Today, Raspberry Shrub is joined on area grocery shelves by Ginger, Blueberry, Cranberry, and Apple Shrub varieties, as well as a large number of marinades, baking mixes, and chutneys.

Tait Farm Apple Cider and Raspberry Shrub Punch

SERVES 20

1 cup Raspberry Shrub
1 gallon apple cider
4 pounds of ice
1 quart club soda

Combine Raspberry Shrub and apple cider in a punch bowl. Stir with a ladle and add ice. Top with club soda and stir to combine.

Tait Farm Strawberry Watermelon Salsa

SERVES 6

1 cup strawberries, diced
1 cup watermelon, diced
1 orange: grate the rind and chop the orange
⅓ cup Ginger Shrub
2 tablespoons chopped fresh mint
2 scallions, finely diced
1 teaspoon snipped chives
¼ teaspoon freshly ground black pepper
  pinch of salt

Mix all ingredients together. Chill one hour, then serve.

Tait Farm
Raspberry Borscht

SERVES 4

1 to 1½ pounds beets

1 quart chicken or vegetable broth

½ cup Tait Farm Raspberry Shrub

    sour cream and diced cucumber for garnish

Scrub and peel the beets. Cut into chunks. Place the beets and broth in a 3-quart pot. Bring to a boil. Reduce heat, cover, and simmer for 45 minutes or until the beets are very tender. Remove from heat and allow to cool somewhat. Strain the beets, reserving the broth. Put beets and some broth in a food processor or blender and puree until smooth. Combine the beet puree with the reserved broth. Add the Raspberry Shrub. Stir well. Chill until cold. Serve in small bowls, garnished with a dollop of sour cream and some diced cucumber.

Tait Farm
Grilled Salmon
with Fruit Salsa

SERVES 6

1½ pounds salmon steaks or other firm fish

1 cup fresh or frozen blueberries

1 avocado, chopped

⅓ cup chopped scallions

1 kiwi, peeled, sliced and quartered

1 tablespoon tamari

2 tablespoons lime juice

¼ cup Ginger Shrub

2 tablespoons oil

1 teaspoon grated ginger

    rind of 1 lime, grated or slivered

    fresh cilantro

    cayenne to taste

Grill salmon steaks over hot coals until done, about 3 minutes on each side. Combine remaining ingredients and serve as a topping for the grilled fish.

Tait Farm
Fresh Raspberry Mango Salsa

MAKES 2½ CUPS

This salsa is delicious with pork, grilled fish or chicken, fajitas, quesadillas, and Mexican salads, or with plain baked tortilla chips.

- 1 cup fresh or frozen raspberries
- 1 mango, peeled and finely diced
- ⅓ cup red bell pepper, minced
- ⅓ cup sweet onion, minced
- 3 tablespoons Raspberry Shrub
- 1 tablespoon lime juice
- 1 teaspoon ground cumin
- ½ teaspoon freshly grated ginger
- ⅛ to ¼ teaspoon cayenne
- pinch of salt
- ¼ cup chopped cilantro or parsley

Combine raspberries, mango, pepper, and onion in a bowl. Mix the Raspberry Shrub, lime juice, cumin, ginger, salt, and pepper. Pour over chopped mixture and let sit to blend the flavors. Add chopped cilantro or parsley right before serving and stir to combine. For a creamy salsa, mix one part fresh salsa with one part sour cream.

Cherry season is short in Central Pennsylvania, and availability is very limited. Farmers' stands or farmers' markets are the best sources. The fruit is just too perishable to make it to the supermarkets. Harner Farm had always been my source for my yearly supply to make into an annual batch of sour cherry jam or a quick torte. When I looked for them one year, however, I learned from Dan Harner that he had removed the trees. "I got tired of feeding the birds," said the farmer, whose stand at Route 26 and Whitehall Road certainly is one of the most visible in the Centre Region area. "We ran into liability problems with our pick-your-own cherries situation because it was dangerous for inexperienced people to be up in the trees."

Native to many parts of Europe and Asia, pie or sour cherries belong to the stone fruit genus Prunus *and the species* P. cerasus. P. avium *is the sweet cherry species. Sour cherries are more hardy than the sweet varieties, and two predominant strains have developed:* amarelles, *with pale red fruit, and* morellos, *with dark red fruit and more acidity.*

Sour Cherry Torte

MAKES ONE 8-INCH CAKE

This is a quick and easy cake that takes maximum advantage of the elusive and delicious cherry with minimum fuss.

- ½ cup unsalted butter
- ¾ cup sugar
- 1 cup unbleached flour, sifted
- 1 teaspoon baking powder
- ½ teaspoon vanilla or almond extract
-    pinch of salt
- 2 eggs
- 1 cup sour cherries, pitted
- 1 tablespoon slivered almonds
- 1 tablespoon sugar

Preheat oven to 350°F. Spray an 8-inch cake pan and line bottom with parchment paper. Cream the butter and sugar together with an electric mixer. Add the flour, baking powder, vanilla or almond extract, and salt. Add the eggs and beat well. Spoon the batter into the pan and place the cherries on top of the batter. Sprinkle lightly with the almonds and sugar. Bake for about 45 minutes, or until inserted toothpick comes out clean. Allow to rest in the pan for 2 minutes, then run a knife around the edge and remove to cooling rack.

Tip

To remove the pits from cherries without destroying the fruit, use a paperclip bent in half so you have two hooked ends. Insert the smaller hooked end into the cherry where it had been connected to the stem and just pull out the pit.

Arts Festival

Sherrie and Charles
Garoian sip Armenian
coffee.

The Central Pennsylvania Festival of the Arts has become a huge street party for town and gown alike in State College the week after the Fourth of July holiday. Artists come from around the country to exhibit their work and enter juried competitions that bring much prestige for the winners. Tens of thousands of people come to town, but it's a crowd very unlike the boisterous football fans that deluge the town in the fall. It's a genteel crowd, with people sporting their most artistic garments to promenade on the streets transformed by hardworking landscapers into pedestrian malls. Multiple stages offer music of many varieties, and orderly concert-goers applaud politely in the rarefied air—that is, until the Earthtones' grand finale on Sunday night, when the town lets down its hair and breathes a great big collective sigh of relief!

During the festival, art is in the spotlight, and townspeople involved in the art world are in focus. Charles Garoian has been involved with the Penn State College of Arts and Architecture and the Palmer Museum of Art since he came to the region in 1986. Both native Californians of Armenian descent, Charles and Sherrie Garoian share the cooking chores when they entertain. And the menu is often a beautiful Armenian feast— perfect to serve to those out-of-towners who visit for the Arts Festival.

Charles Garoian's Skewered Lamb

SERVES 8

- 1 leg of lamb (5 to 6 pounds), bone and fat removed
- 2 medium red onions, minced
- ¼ cup fresh parsley, chopped
- 2 teaspoons black pepper
- 1 teaspoon salt
- 1 clove garlic, crushed
- 2 cups red Burgundy wine

Cut lamb into 1½-inch cubes. Combine remaining ingredients with the lamb cubes and marinate in a glass, enamel, or acrylic container for two days in the refrigerator. Thread meat on skewers and barbecue over hot coals or broil in oven until meat is medium. Overcooking dries out the kebabs. This recipe is also good for chicken, using white wine instead of the red and reducing the marinating time to one overnight.

Sherrie Garoian's Rice Pilaf

SERVES 4

- 2 tablespoons olive oil
- ½ cup vermicelli noodles, broken into 1-inch lengths
- 2 tablespoons butter or margarine
- 1 cup long-grain rice
- 2 cups chicken broth (one 14½-ounce can plus water to make 2 cups)

Heat oil and brown vermicelli. Add butter and melt. Add rice and stir to coat. Add chicken broth and bring to full boil for 2 minutes. Turn heat to low, cover, and cook approximately 20 minutes. Turn off heat and let stand 5 minutes. Mix and serve.

Celebration Cake

SERVES 12

Here is a showstopper of a dessert that allows the baker to create a work of art worthy of arts-conscious guests.

SPONGE CAKE
(makes two 9-inch cake layers):

6 eggs, separated

1 cup sugar

2 tablespoons hot water

1 tablespoon lemon juice

½ teaspoon vanilla

1 cup plus 2 tablespoons cake flour

1 teaspoon baking powder

¼ teaspoon salt

1 stick unsalted butter, melted and cooled

FILLING:

3 cups sweet cherries, pitted, or 3 cups raspberries or blueberries

3 cups vanilla yogurt

FROSTING:

24 ounces cream cheese, softened

¾ cup powdered sugar

zest from 1 lemon

FOR ASSEMBLY:

⅓ cup Triple Sec

⅔ cup orange juice, freshly squeezed and strained

½ cup melted cherry jelly

1 starfruit, sliced

8 strawberries, halved if large

8 green grapes, halved

8 red grapes, halved

1 plum, cut into slices

1 kiwi, peeled and sliced

1 orange, peeled and sectioned

sprigs of mint or scented geranium

Prepare two 9-inch cake pans by lining with parchment paper. Preheat oven to 350°F. Place egg yolks in metal bowl over simmering water and beat with whisk until smooth. Add sugar and continue beating until mixture lightens and reaches 100°F on an instant-read thermometer.

Warm a large mixing bowl with hot water, dry thoroughly, then place the mixture of egg yolk and sugar in it. Beat with a paddle until the mixture is light yellow and has increased in volume.

In small measuring cup, combine the hot water (use the water the yolks were simmering over) with the lemon juice and vanilla. Sift together the cake flour, baking powder, and salt. Beat egg whites until soft peaks form. Heat the butter in a microwave and allow to cool.

Gently fold the flour mixture into the egg-yolk mixture to make a batter. Fold the egg whites into batter with a spatula. Remove one cup of the batter and combine it with the melted butter. Add the combined mixture to the remaining batter and fold to combine.

Pour the batter into prepared pans and bake in upper third of preheated oven for 22 to 25 minutes, or until golden brown and an inserted toothpick comes out clean. Allow cakes to remain in pans for a few minutes, then loosen edge with knife and cool on cake racks.

When cool, split the layers horizontally. Combine the Triple Sec and the orange juice and brush the cut sides with the liquid.

Combine filling ingredients and use one-third to fill each layer. Spread the last third on top of one layer and place the other filled layer on top of that. Brush top of cake with the melted jelly.

Whip the cream cheese and add the powdered sugar and lemon zest. Place the cake on a footed serving platter and frost with the cream cheese mixture. Arrange the fruit and herbs all over the exterior of the cake in a pleasing pattern, and brush the tops of the fruit with the remaining melted jelly. Chill thoroughly before cutting so all layers settle together.

Tip

Chill cake before frosting. Keep cream-cheese frosting at room temperature. Spread a very thin layer on the cake, taking care not to get any loose cake crumbs in the frosting bowl. Chill the cake with the thin basecoat before finishing with the rest of the room-temperature frosting.

Summer's Bounty : Corn

The height of summer in Central Pennsylvania is measured by the towering cornstalks that dominate the horizon. Hike in any direction and you are likely to find yourself in the middle of a cornfield dwarfed by staunch, orderly rows of the tasseled "king of the grains." Native to the Americas and often held in religious awe by ancient peoples, corn is botanically a unique giant grass. It is classified in the genus Zea *and, aside from the Central America weed* teosinte *it has no close relatives. Corn's male and female elements are separate flower clusters on each plant: the male, commonly known as the tassel, at the top of the plant, and the female, the short, heavy growths (the "ears"), which are really greatly condensed side branches. The ears are protected by special leaves known as husks that have the long styles of the female flowers protruding from them (the silks). Corn pollen is carried by wind from the tassels on top to the silks of the ears. For this reason, corn is planted in rows to ensure pollination.*

Corn, considered a "heavy feeder," is highly nutritious, pulling nourishment from the soil and sunshine. Native Americans taught the settlers their growing techniques—fertilizing each seed planted with a dead fish, and using the cornstalks as support for bean vines in an early effort at companion planting—and how to eat it. Squaws built fires beside the cornfields and boiled water for the freshly picked ears, astounding the settlers who had never seen anything like fresh corn being eaten. The Indians also taught the colonists the aboriginal method of pounding parched corn into meal for bread and porridge. Succotash, made with fresh or dried corn and beans, became the national dish.

In the United States about one-third of all plowed land is planted in corn. Only a minor fraction of the crop reaches the ultimate consumer as a recognizable corn product, however, attesting to its versatility. On the average, every American uses about eight ears of corn every day of the year. It comes in the form of beef, bacon, ham, lard, milk, eggs, salad oil, candy bars, soft drinks, bakery goods, ice cream, alcoholic beverages, glue, laundry starch, vitamin tablets, fireworks, and face powder.

Farmers' markets and roadside stands are the best sources for local corn in the summer—unless you are lucky enough to have your own growing in the backyard. By far the most popular way to eat corn in the summer is corn on the cob.

Corn on the Cob

BOILING:

Submerge shucked whole ears of corn in boiling water and bring back to a boil. Place a lid on the pot and remove it from the heat. Depending on freshness, the corn will be cooked after 3 to 5 minutes. The fresher the corn, the less cooking it requires. Do not add salt to the cooking water, but adding ¼ teaspoon sugar for each quart of water can benefit corn that is more than an hour old.

STEAMING:

Shucked whole ears of corn can be steamed for 5 to 10 minutes over 2 inches of rapidly boiling water, depending on the age of the corn.

GRILLING:

Corn can be grilled by peeling down the husks and carefully removing the silk. Pull the husks back up and tie the top together with string. Soak prepared ears in cold water for 10 minutes and shake dry before laying the ears over hot coals. Grill for 25 to 30 minutes, turning frequently until husks are evenly browned.

Tait Farm Chipotle Gazpacho

MAKES 10 CUPS

- 46 ounces tomato juice
- 1 cup Tait Farm Chipotle Sauce
- 1½ cups corn, fresh or canned
- 1½ cups cucumber, diced
- 1½ cups fresh tomatoes, peeled, seeded and diced
- 1 small clove of garlic, pressed through a garlic mincer
- 2 scallions, finely minced
- 2 teaspoons ground cumin
- ⅛ teaspoon cayenne pepper

Combine all ingredients in a large container. Chill at least 3 hours or overnight. Serve very cold, garnished with some chopped avocado or cucumber.

Tip

For best flavor, corn should be cooked immediately after picking. If cooking is delayed for even an hour, part of the sugar in the kernels will have turned to starch. When it is necessary to delay cooking, ears should be chilled immediately after picking and stored in their husks in the coldest part of the refrigerator.

Corn Fritters

MAKES 2 DOZEN

These were my dad's favorite "vegetable."

1¼ cups flour

2¼ teaspoons baking powder

1 teaspoon salt

1 egg, yolk separated from the white

¾ cup milk

1½ teaspoons corn oil

2 cups corn kernels, cut from 4 ears of cooked corn

oil for deep frying

maple syrup or sugar for sprinkling

Sift together the flour, baking powder, and salt into a medium-size bowl. In a small bowl, combine the egg yolk, milk, and corn oil. Mix the liquids into the dry ingredients to create a batter. Beat the egg white with a wire whisk until stiff, then fold into the batter. Gently stir in the corn.

Drop by the tablespoonful into deep-frying oil preheated to 375°F. Fry until the fritters are puffed and golden brown, turning once. This should take approximately 5 minutes. Drain the fritters on paper toweling and serve at once, with maple syrup or a sprinkling of sugar if desired.

Corn Chowder

SERVES 4 TO 6

2 medium waxy potatoes, diced

pinch of salt

¼ cup onion, minced

2 tablespoons butter

3 ears of raw corn, shucked and kernels removed (or substitute 2 cups corn kernels)

2 cups milk

½ cup half-and-half

sprig of fresh thyme or a pinch of dried thyme

salt and pepper

In a 2-quart saucepan, cook potatoes in just enough salted water to cover for about 20 minutes, or until tender. Sauté onion in butter until translucent, then add to the potatoes along with the corn, milk, half-and-half, and thyme. Simmer for 20 to 30 minutes, stirring occasionally. Remove thyme and season to taste with salt and pepper.

Harmony Joseph's
Thai Shrimp and Corn Cakes

MAKES 35

Harmony Joseph (see Winter, page 109) serves these as a summertime savory at teatime in her garden.

3 cups fresh corn kernels (about 5 ears)

2 eggs, beaten

2 tablespoons cornstarch

2 teaspoons sugar

2 teaspoons nam pla (fish sauce)
or ½ teaspoon salt

¼ pound raw shrimp, peeled and minced

2 cloves garlic, minced

⅓ cup finely chopped fresh tomato

2 tablespoons minced pickled jalapeños

¼ cup fresh chives, minced

¼ cup fresh cilantro, minced

2 tablespoons fresh basil (Thai basil,
if possible), chopped

fresh pepper to taste

cooking spray or canola oil for frying

Remove the corn from the cob and measure 3 cups. Combine the beaten eggs, cornstarch, sugar, and nam pla or salt in a medium bowl and mix well. Add the corn to the mixture. Add the shrimp, garlic, tomato, jalapeños, chives, cilantro, basil, and pepper. Mix together.

Heat a nonstick skillet to medium-high and spray with cooking spray or coat with a small amount of canola oil. Use a ladle to measure out the cakes in 2½-inch-diameter circles. Cook until golden brown on one side, flip, and continue cooking the other side. Serve warm.

Cook's Note

Nam pla is fish sauce that is used as a seasoning in many Thai and Vietnamese dishes.

Tip

If the corn is very fresh and sweet, you may need to add another 1 or 2 tablespoons of cornstarch so the mixture holds together.

Scott Storll's Roasted Corn Salsa

MAKES 6 CUPS

Another use for the locally made Seth's Hot Sauce (see page 23). This salsa is good served with corn chips, grilled chicken, grilled pork, and fish. Pass more hot sauce on the side for the daring ones.

    6 ears of corn
    1 tablespoon olive oil
    1 red or green pepper, roasted
    4 tablespoons fresh cilantro, chopped
    1 teaspoon dried oregano
    3 scallions, minced
    1 tablespoon garlic, minced
      salt and pepper to taste
    1 to 10 tablespoons Seth's Hot Sauce, red variety

Cut kernels off the cob and dry roast the corn over medium-high heat in large nonstick frying pan, stirring constantly so that it doesn't burn. The corn should be lightly browned and somewhat cooked. Place the corn in a large mixing bowl to come to room temperature.

Roast the pepper and remove the skin. Dice the pepper the same size as the corn kernels and add to the corn along with the cilantro, the scallions, and the garlic. In a large bowl, mix all the ingredients together and season with salt and pepper to taste. Add the hot sauce one tablespoon at a time, tasting after each addition, until reaching the desired amount of heat.

Summer's Bounty : Tomatoes

Central Pennsylvania's rich soil supports many different vegetables in home gardens in the summer, but none as ubiquitous as the bright-red Lycopersicon esculentum. *Tomatoes are the most popular homegrown garden vegetable, because there is a world of difference between a supermarket tomato, which is picked green so it won't bruise in shipping, and a tomato that is vine-ripened in the garden.*

Garden tomatoes take six days from the first blush of color to peak ripeness. Technically, tomatoes are ripe when the plant sugar stops moving into the fruit. At this point they have their maximum vitamin A content of 766 international units, a vitamin C content of 32 milligrams, and 273 milligrams of potassium per 100-gram portion (about one 4-ounce tomato). All this goodness costs only about 25 calories. If the skin is consumed, tomatoes also have a lot of fiber.

Native to tropical America, where they are perennials, tomatoes were a part of the South American and Central American indigenous diet; their name is derived from the Mexican Indian name, tomatl. *Revered for years as an aphrodisiac, tomatoes were called "love apples" by the French. However, the English and consequently the early New World colonists considered them poisonous and grew them for ornamental purposes only. In 1781 Thomas Jefferson had them planted in his garden and their culinary use spread northward. The first varieties cultivated were ribbed, some of them red, some yellow. Smooth, round tomatoes were developed in the nineteenth century. Today, many specialty growers are reverting to the heirloom varieties that have unusual shapes and colors and explode with flavor.*

Bruschetta

SERVES I

Our favorite use for tomatoes in season is bruschetta, a simple Italian peasant snack that is the perfect combination of texture and flavor. I first discovered this on a trip to Italy in 1985. We stayed with friends who took us to their local restaurant, which they nicknamed "Smokey's" because of the thick cloud of smoke that hung over the upper third of the dining room. All the cooking was done over an open fire and included thick slices of crusty Italian bread toasted on both sides then rubbed with whole cloves of fresh garlic, drizzled with virgin olive oil, topped with a thick slice of tomato, and sprinkled with salt and pepper. For added pizzazz, tuck a leaf of basil under the tomato or sprinkle with fresh oregano flowers.

    thick slice of crusty Italian bread

    peeled clove of garlic

    best-quality olive oil

I thick slice of perfectly ripe tomato

    kosher or sea salt

    freshly ground pepper

Grill the bread over hot coals on both sides. Depending on how much you like garlic, rub one or both sides of the bread with the garlic clove. If you have an Italian olive-oil can with a very narrow spout, you can drizzle some oil over one side of the bread; otherwise, put some olive oil in a small bowl and use a pastry brush to brush one side of the bread. Put the tomato slice on the bread and sprinkle with salt and pepper.

Fresh Tomato Sauce with Fettuccini

SERVES 4 TO 6

1 pound fettuccini (fresh, if possible)
½ cup freshly grated Parmesan cheese

SAUCE:

2 pounds very ripe tomatoes, washed
1 small onion, minced
1 clove garlic, minced
½ cup fresh basil, chopped
½ cup olive oil
salt and freshly ground pepper, to taste

Bring 5 quarts of water to a boil and drop the tomatoes in, removing them with a slotted spoon after 1 minute. Remove water from heat and cover until time to cook the pasta. Place blanched tomatoes in a bowl of cold water to stop the cooking. When cool enough to handle, peel, seed, and coarsely chop them. In a large bowl, combine the chopped tomatoes with the onion, garlic, basil, oil, salt, and pepper. Allow to sit at room temperature for one hour before serving.

Bring the water back to a boil and cook pasta until al dente. Drain. In the large bowl with the tomato sauce, toss the hot pasta until fully combined. Serve immediately with the Parmesan cheese.

Tip

This dish is good hot, cold, or at room temperature, so it is perfect for summer entertaining.

Ratatouille Niçoise

SERVES 4 TO 6

3 cups onion, chopped

½ cup olive oil

3 tomatoes, peeled, seeded, and chopped

4 medium zucchini, sliced

1 medium eggplant, peeled and sliced

3 peppers, any color, halved, seeded, and cut into strips

1 garlic clove, minced

1 bouquet garni (a sprig of parsley, thyme, and a bay leaf tied together)

salt and pepper to taste

Cook the onions in the olive oil over low heat in a large pan for about 10 minutes, or until they are softened. Add the tomatoes and cook for a few more minutes. Add the zucchini, eggplant, peppers, garlic, bouquet garni, salt, and pepper. Cover and simmer over low heat for one hour, or until the vegetables have released their liquid and are tender and blended. To reduce the liquid, remove the lid and continue cooking for another 20 to 30 minutes.

Cook's Notes

Selecting: If at all possible, choose red ripe tomatoes that yield to gentle pressure when you touch them. Tomatoes should ripen on the vine.

Storage: Fruit that is picked but not quite ripe should be kept between 65° and 75°F in light, but not direct sunlight, positioned with the stem-end down. A tomato will ripen this way in five or six days but never really have the depth of flavor or the full nutritive value of its vine-ripened counterparts. Tomatoes can be coaxed into ripening more quickly by placing them in a brown paper bag with an apple, which produces ethylene, the same gas naturally produced by tomatoes to ripen themselves.

Canning: Tomatoes can be dried, frozen, or canned, but canning is preferable. Today's low-acid varieties, however, necessitate adding an acid to the product, typically citric acid or lemon juice.

Drying: Tomatoes are most effectively dried in a dehydrator due to the high moisture content. The fruit must not be overripe or it will tend to mold. Choose firm fruit at the peak of maturity. Slice ⅜ inch thick from top to bottom and arrange the slices in a single layer on a drying tray with room between the slices for air circulation. When dry, they can be put into heavy-duty plastic bags or packed into jars and covered with olive oil, like expensive Italian sun-dried tomatoes.

Freezing: Tomatoes can be frozen whole to be used in cooking later, but they take up a lot of storage space in the freezer because of all the water in the raw product. They are not suitable for anything but a cooked tomato product after having been frozen.

Summer's Bounty : Peaches

Peaches, sometimes called the "queen of fruits," are ranked number four in popularity in America, after apples, oranges, and grapes. The flavor of a perfectly ripe peach is the province of late summer, however, because the fruit is highly perishable and what is shipped to the supermarkets at other times of the year is necessarily hard and underripe. Peach season is eagerly awaited by peach pie enthusiasts in the Centre Region. Lynn Schlow, a State College resident, makes a very rich open-face peach pie that is good either warm or cold.

Lynn Schlow's Peach Pie

MAKES 1 PIE

pastry for a 9- or 10-inch pie, unbaked

4 large peaches

¼ pound unsalted butter, melted

1 teaspoon vanilla

½ cup sugar

½ tablespoon of flour

½ tablespoon of cornstarch

2 egg yolks

Preheat oven to 375°F. Peel and slice peaches into the pastry crust. Combine melted butter, vanilla, sugar, flour, cornstarch, and egg yolks in a food processor and process until smooth. Pour over the peaches and bake for 45 minutes, until the crust and the top of the pie are golden brown.

Peach Melba Jam

MAKES 6 HALF-PINTS

7 large unblemished peaches, peeled, pitted, and chopped (about 6 cups)

2 tablespoons fresh lemon juice

5 cups sugar

1 pint raspberries, rinsed and drained

Place the peaches, lemon juice, and sugar in a heavy saucepan. Slowly bring to a boil over low heat, stirring occasionally until the sugar dissolves, 10 to 15 minutes. Increase heat to moderate and boil, stirring occasionally, for 20 minutes. Remove from the heat and add the raspberries. Return to heat and boil, stirring constantly, for 5 minutes. Skim off any foam.

Remove from the heat and test for thickness by dabbing about ½ teaspoon of the jam onto a chilled plate and placing it in the freezer for 3 minutes. Push the jam gently with your finger. If the surface wrinkles, the jam is ready for processing. If it does not, the jam is too thin. Return to the heat, boil for another 5 minutes, then retest.

When the jam is properly thickened, ladle into six sterile, hot, dry half-pint jars and fill them within ¼ inch of the top. Wipe the rims with a clean, damp cloth. Place the lids on the jars and tighten the screw bands. Process in a boiling water bath for 15 minutes.

Tip

This is an old-fashioned recipe without added pectin. Depending on the amount of pectin in the fruit, it may be runny, but it makes a delicious sauce. If you want to guarantee a very firm product, use commercial pectin and follow the package directions.

Cook's Note

See directions that come with the canning jars and lids and follow the correct procedure for sterilizing the jars before filling.

Preservation Time

The abundance of many Central Pennsylvania gardens is frequently "put up" in a time-honored way—by canning. It might not be exactly what you feel like doing on a hot summer day—trimming 10 pounds of green beans or blanching 40 pounds of tomatoes or shucking 4 dozen ears of corn—but it's a task that can't be postponed for long.

Home-canned foods preserve the bounty of the garden.

Between 1984 and 1989 Dr. Gerald Kuhn, a professor and nationally known authority on home canning, headed the USDA Center for Excellence in Home Food Preservation on the Penn State main campus. It was the first facility in the United States federally funded for evaluating old and developing new techniques. A nearly half-million-dollar grant authorized research into canning methods for the first time in thirty years. Research conducted in the 1970s had indicated problems with home-canned foods. Grandma's old-fashioned methods did not take into account technological changes in the jars, lids, and pressure canners available. Vegetables themselves had changed. New hybrid types of low-acid tomatoes necessitated a reevaluation of common practices.

With increasing concern about food additives, there was also increased demand from the public about just how to preserve food properly and to prevent spoilage and food-borne illness. The method used to disseminate the new guidelines to the people was the Master Food Preserver program administered by the county extension service. Six master food preservers were certified when I took the course, which taught the latest methods of home canning with the specific purpose of sharing knowledge with the general public. There was no charge for the course; our "payback" was thirty hours of community service. MFPs made themselves available for canning questions during the evening and weekend hours that the extension service was closed—times when most people were actually doing the canning. Some MFPs did hands-on workshops and special presentations to clubs and groups. We were an extension of the extension service.

Pickled Corn Pepper Relish

MAKES 9 PINTS

- 10 cups fresh whole-kernel corn (16 to 20 medium ears) or six 10-ounce packages of frozen corn
- 2½ cups sweet red peppers, diced
- 2½ cups sweet green peppers, diced
- 2½ cups celery, chopped
- 1¼ cups onion, diced
- 1¾ cups sugar
- 5 cups vinegar (5 percent acidity)
- 2½ teaspoons canning or pickling salt
- 1½ teaspoons celery seeds
- 2½ tablespoons dry mustard
- 1¼ teaspoons turmeric

Boil ears of corn for 3 to 5 minutes, depending on freshness. Plunge into cold water to stop the cooking. Cut the kernels from the cob (or use frozen corn that has been defrosted under cool running water).

Combine peppers, celery, onions, sugar, vinegar, salt, and celery seeds in a large saucepot. Bring to a boil and simmer for 5 minutes, stirring occasionally. Ladle out ½ cup of this simmered mixture, mix in the mustard and turmeric until blended, then return to larger saucepot along with the corn. Simmer another 5 minutes.

Fill hot sterilized jars with the hot mixture, leaving ½ inch of headspace. Adjust lids and process for 16 minutes in a boiling water bath at 1,000 to 2,000 feet altitude.

Pickled Dilly Beans

MAKES 4 PINTS

- 2 pounds fresh, tender green or yellow beans (4 to 5 inches long)
- 4 heads fresh dill
- 4 cloves garlic
- ¼ cup canning or pickling salt
- 2 cups white vinegar (5 percent acidity)
- 2 cups water
- ½ teaspoon hot red-pepper flakes (optional)

Wash and trim ends from beans. In each presterilized pint jar, place 1 head of dill and 1 clove of garlic. Pack whole raw beans uniformly in jars, leaving ½ inch of headspace. Trim beans to ensure proper fit, if necessary. Combine salt, vinegar, water, and pepper flakes and bring to a boil. Add hot solution to beans, leaving ½ inch of headspace. Adjust lids and process for 6 minutes raw at 1,000 to 2,000 feet altitude in a boiling water bath.

Another use for tomatoes in Central Pennsylvania gardens, especially when there is an unexpected frost warning and all the vegetables need to be harvested suddenly, is a Green Tomato Chutney. Made and championed by local grande dame Grace Holderman, the condiment is offered at Centre Furnace Mansion, where she serves on the Mary Irving Thompson Sideboard Committee, which organizes fund-raising events.

"The original recipe, for Green Tomato and Lime Conserve, came from Shirley and Bob Bernreuter, but I call it Never-the-Same-Twice Chutney or Sub-Limed Chutney or Major Gra-a-a-a-ace's Chutney," explained the diminutive and dynamic woman. "Old friends give me their green tomatoes at the end of the growing season, and I buy limes during the summer when they are plentiful and inexpensive, slice them, and freeze them. The mixture is easy to put together and smells heavenly when it is simmering on the stove."

Lately Grace has branched into other chutney domains, cantaloupe mixed with apple, and a black cherry variety, but the green tomato version is her mainstay. A group of her women friends known as the Fearless Fabulous Fivesome meets frequently to socialize, and when it's Grace's turn to entertain she serves her chutney her favorite way. First she spreads a Bremner wafer with a thin layer of natural peanut butter, then tops it with a dollop of the chutney. "I put on as much as the cracker will hold. It's always a big hit," she says.

Chutney is a type of Indian condiment that derives from the Sanskrit word "chatney (to lick). Enormously versatile, chutney can be made from almost any combination of fruits and usually uses a few aromatic vegetables like onion or garlic. The preservation of chutney is guaranteed by combining the natural fruit sugar and added sugar with the vinegar, an acid. Brown sugar and red-wine or cider vinegar contribute to the characteristic dark color and deep rich flavor of chutney. It keeps indefinitely if stored in a covered container in the refrigerator, and may be put up in sterile jars and processed in a boiling water bath for longer storage or to give as gifts. Since it is cooked, it can also be frozen.

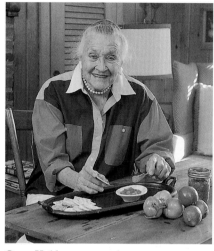

Grace Holderman spreads her Green Tomato Chutney.

Grace Holderman's Never-the-Same-Twice Green Tomato Chutney

MAKES 4 CUPS

People's personalities come through when they write a recipe. Grace lends her flair for the dramatic in her rendition of the recipe.

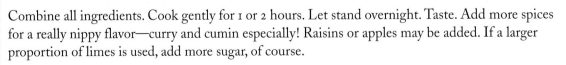

- 6 cups chopped green tomatoes
- 3 cups limes, cut into quarters and sliced
- 2 cups sugar
- ½ teaspoon cinnamon
- ¼ teaspoon—or more!—EACH ginger, clove, allspice, nutmeg
- 1½ teaspoons salt
- 5 or 6 shakes EACH garlic powder and onion powder
- ½ teaspoon mustard seeds
- 1 teaspoon dried sweet-pepper flakes
- ¼ teaspoon red-pepper flakes or cayenne
- 1 teaspoon—or more—curry powder
- ½ to 1 teaspoon ground cumin
- 1 to 2 tablespoons vinegar

Combine all ingredients. Cook gently for 1 or 2 hours. Let stand overnight. Taste. Add more spices for a really nippy flavor—curry and cumin especially! Raisins or apples may be added. If a larger proportion of limes is used, add more sugar, of course.

Japanese Influence

Masaya (pronounced "Masa") Matsui, a native of Japan, lives in Warrior's Mark with his wife, Sue, and their two children, Max and Miya. Sue, born and raised in Centre County, met Masaya while she was living in New York City. Trips to visit Sue's family in the State College area, and to her grandmother's farm in Beech Creek, convinced the couple to move to Central Pennsylvania when they married.

When not working as a cook at the Gamble Mill or preparing sushi for special events, Masaya grows shiitake mushrooms on their fifty-acre farm. However, he uses the method his family used in their remote village in Japan, where earthquakes are common. He inoculates living oak logs with mushroom spores, which cure for a year in a breezy, wooded area on his farm. When he wants the logs to produce, he soaks them in water and brings them into the barn near his house so he can tend them constantly. Heeding his grandfather's advice that "shiitakes like earthquakes," Masaya uses a long, heavy mallet to tap the logs and simulate the vibration of an earthquake in the seismically stable Centre Region.

Masaya Matsui harvests shiitake mushrooms with his son Max.

Masaya Matsui's Miso Soup

SERVES 2

3 cups water

1 3-inch piece of kombu (seaweed)

2 shiitake mushrooms, sliced

1½ tablespoons dark miso

1 tablespoon scallion, sliced

3 tablespoons tofu, cut into ½-inch dice

optional additions: 3 tablespoons dried bonito flakes; 8 dried anchovies; ½ cup of various vegetables such as okra, Napa cabbage, cooked new potato, stinging nettle, fiddlehead fern, or fresh, young bamboo shoots

Combine water and kombu in a small saucepan. Bring to a boil, then discard the kombu. Add the mushrooms and reduce the heat to a simmer. Add the miso, the scallion, and the tofu and heat thoroughly. Add any additional optional ingredients desired.

Tips

Store shiitakes in a paper bag, never in plastic. They will keep this way for about a month and will only dry out as they age, so they can be reconstituted with water.

Trim the stem of shiitakes so the stem is even with the cap. The stems are tough but can be used to flavor soups, stocks, or broth.

Never eat shiitake mushrooms raw. They are not harmful, but they don't taste good unless they are cooked.

Clean shiitakes by wiping them with a damp paper towel to remove any dirt.

Masaya Matsui's Shiitake Mushrooms

SERVES 4

This Japanese treatment of shiitake mushrooms is perfect for including in a rolled sushi presentation, or just for serving on top of rice.

12 shiitake mushrooms, sliced into thin strips

1 cup water

2 tablespoons soy sauce

2 tablespoons sake

1½ tablespoons sugar

Combine all ingredients and cook until the mushrooms are tender.

Grange Fair Time

Late summer is Grange Fair time in Central Pennsylvania, and Centre Hall is the site for the annual meeting of the Pomona Grange, a county-wide farmers' association with 125-year-old roots. The last tented residential encampment in the country, the fair is like a big family reunion, with hundreds of family units closely packed onto 212 acres covered with 950 one-room tents and 1,350 travel trailers.

Seven days long, the fair attracts droves of additional day visitors who come for a variety of reasons. Some come to appreciate the exhibits—the biggest pumpkin and Hubbard squash; the best jar of zucchini pickles; the blue-ribbon-winning pies, cakes, and tarts; quilts, crafts, and floral arrangements—the bounty of the farm in glorious fruition. Some come to watch the animal-judging or the tractor-pulls, to hear the country music in the grandstand, or to see the farm machinery vendors with their gleaming brand-new equipment. Some bring their children to wait in long lines for amusement rides. Many come for the food alone—Scott's roast pork sandwiches, the sausage sandwiches, the halupki and pierogies, the farmer-size country platters, the delicate funnel cakes, warm sticky-buns, and flaky apple dumplings served with hot cinnamon sauce and vanilla ice cream.

Each year a baking contest is organized by the statewide grange, which sends a particular recipe to use to all the home economics chairpersons of the various units. Criteria used in the judging are appearance, color, texture, and flavor. The contest in 1985 was for Shoofly Cake and proved that the skill of the baker can manipulate even a six-ingredient recipe. Edith Stine of the Port Matilda Grange took first place for her version, crediting Port Matilda water for giving her the edge.

A tent camper doesn't mind a lack of privacy in the home away from home.

Grange Shoofly Cake

MAKES 12 OR 16 SERVINGS

Shoofly cake is a traditional Pennsylvania Dutch unfrosted cake, also called a "dunking" cake or coffee cake. The cake derives from one the most popular of Pennsylvania Dutch pies, the shoofly pie. Although origins of the intriguing name have never been authenticated, various theories exist. The word might be a corruption of the French word choufleur *(cauliflower), since the texture of its crumb-besprinkled surface resembles a head of cauliflower. Another theory is the more practical (and therefore more Pennsylvania Dutch) explanation that "shoo fly" is what the housewife said as she waved her hand over the pie as it cooled on an open windowsill.*

   4 cups flour

   2 cups brown sugar

   ¾ cup shortening

   2 cups boiling water

   1 cup molasses

   1 tablespoon baking soda

Preheat oven to 350°F. Spray or grease and flour a 9 x 13 baking pan. Combine flour and brown sugar in large bowl. Cut in shortening, and remove 1 cup of the crumb mixture to reserve for a topping. Add water, molasses, and baking soda to the remaining crumb mixture in the bowl and mix. Pour into the prepared pan and scatter the reserved 1 cup of crumbs on the top. Bake at 350°F for 45 minutes, or until a toothpick inserted comes out clean.

Credits

Photographs:

CDT/Dick Brown: pages 83, 94

Lois Chavern: pages 111, 162

CDT/Steve Coon: pages 37, 98, 153

CDT/Tom Fedor: pages 138, 173

CDT/Craig Houtz: page 56

Tom King: pages vii, 59, 111, 167

Alan Klein: pages 16, 34, 72, 76, 81, 85, 109, 121, 151, 183, 213

CDT/Michelle Morton Klein: pages 32, 68, 124, 126, 160, 180, 181, 215

CDT/Pat Little: pages 7, 9, 24, 44, 50, 52, 66, 102, 104, 119, 135, 136, 140, 154, 155, 165, 196, 211

CDT/Robin Loznak: pages 11, 26, 27, 92, 142

Bill Mak: page 174

CDT/Michelle Mott: page 106

Carolyn Smith: pages 187, 217

CDT/Jim Staebler: page 30

Recipes:

Recipes on the following pages have been previously published in the *Centre Daily Times*:

Fall: pages 8, 9, 10, 12, 19, 20, 21, 22, 23, 25, 27, 30, 31, 33, 38, 44, 45, 48, 49, 51, 53, 57

Winter: pages 65, 67, 69, 70, 71, 74, 79, 82, 84, 86, 89, 90, 93, 96, 97, 99, 100, 103, 105, 107, 108

Spring: pages 118, 120, 122, 124, 126, 129, 135, 137, 139, 141, 143, 145, 146, 147, 148, 149, 150, 152, 153, 157, 158, 159, 161, 166

Summer: pages 173, 175, 176, 179, 181, 182, 184, 187, 191, 192, 197, 202, 206, 207, 208, 210, 212, 214, 216, 218

The chronology on page 151 is based primarily on information provided by the Pennsylvania Fish and Boat Commission.

Name Index

Recipe Index